THE COMPLETE GUIDE TO
BOXING
FITNESS

THE COMPLETE GUIDE TO
BOXING
FITNESS

A non-contact boxing training manual

Hilary Lissenden

B L O O M S B U R Y
LONDON · NEW DELHI · NEW YORK · SYDNEY

Published by Bloomsbury Publishing Plc
50 Bedford Square
London WC1B 3DP
www.bloomsbury.com

First edition 2013

ISBN (print): 978 1 4081 9033 3
ISBN (Epub): 978 1 4729 0280 1
ISBN (Epdf): 978 1 4729 0281 8

A CIP catalogue record for this book is available from the British Library.

Acknowledgements
Cover photograph © Shutterstock
Inside photographs © Grant Pritchard, Shutterstock and Getty
Illustrations by David Gardner and Tom Croft
Designed by James Watson
Commissioned by Charlotte Croft
Edited by Sarah Cole

This book is produced using paper that is made from wood grown in managed, sustainable forests. It is natural, renewable and recyclable. The logging and manufacturing processes conform to the environmental regulations of the country of origin.

Typeset in 10.75pt on 14pt Adobe Caslon by seagulls.net

Printed and bound in India by Replika Press Pvt Ltd

10 9 8 7 6 5 4 3 2 1

CONTENTS

PREFACE

I'd like to say that boxing has always been part of my life, but it wouldn't be true. I came to the sport relatively late, in my thirties. Bored of anodyne workouts, and overweight post-childbirth, I walked off the street on a whim into Clinton McKenzie's boxing fitness gym and into a whole new world.

The 'get fit, not hit' mantra may be a cliché today, but at that time the idea of introducing traditional boxing techniques to the general public, without the contact and therefore the inherent risk, was pioneering. I took to the training from day one. Within eight weeks I had lost weight and toned up. People noticed; I felt great.

But boxing training is hard work, and even harder was taking it further, into the realms of competition. I was too old to apply for an amateur or professional licence, and it was almost impossible for women to be taken seriously in the male-dominated boxing arena. So I turned to coaching. I supplemented my personal training diploma with a course specialising in focus pad techniques, and started to pass on the boxing fitness revelation to my clients. Today, as a qualified coach and judge for the Amateur Boxing Association, I see the physical and therapeutic benefits of boxing training every day.

It delighted me on all kinds of levels to witness the groundbreaking triumph of the female boxers at London 2012. I'd like to say I know what the road was like for them, but it wouldn't be true – although I do have an inkling of what kept them battling on, against heavy odds. Boxing has a particular allure, which has at last become accessible to everyone, clients and trainers alike. It's my hope that this book will help you make the most of the professional and personal opportunities it affords. Most of all, I'd like it to encourage you to innovate in your career, adding boxing fitness to your repertoire with an original stamp that is truly your own.

Hilary Lissenden
May 2013

A word from the ABA

"BOX" is the new Amateur Boxing Association REPS accredited training programme for the fitness market.

Training will be rolled out for suitably qualified teachers in schools, colleges and universities, youth workers and sports coaches as well as group and personal trainers in the fitness industry.

The training is based on quality glove and pad work that would be used to prepare boxers for competition but is easily transferable to be used as a means for a general keep fit workout based on boxing movements.

INTRODUCTION

BOXING FITNESS AND THE EXERCISE PROFESSIONAL

BOXING TODAY – PUTTING IT ALL IN CONTEXT

1

GIRLS IN GLOVES? 'THAT'S MADE MY DAY!'

Among the many remarkable events and achievements of the London 2012 Olympic Games, people around the world were charmed and delighted by one petite, Leeds-born lass who fought her way to sporting history in the boxing ring.

Standing only 1.64m and weighing less than 51kg, Britain's Nicola Adams became the first ever woman to win an Olympic boxing gold, as she beat the Chinese world number one, Ren Cancan, by a resounding 16 points to 7 in the flyweight division.

The ripples of admiration that spread outwards from Nicola's performance were not just for the victory itself; nor were they for the novelty of watching a woman box. They were mostly for the sheer level of skill, fitness and discipline exhibited by this diminutive figure on the royal blue stage of the East London arena.

Girls in gloves? Even the most die-hard doubters could not deny the accuracy and speed of Adams' hands, the balance and virtuosity of her footwork, and the focus, determination and courage that together served to make her dream of 15 years become a reality – qualities known collectively in boxing as 'heart'.

And if all that wasn't enough to win people over, Nicola's post-bout interview surely did the trick. Asked how it felt to make sporting history, she replied endearingly in her broad Yorkshire accent: 'That's made my day, that has.'

BACK IN BUSINESS

The ratification of women's boxing as a full Olympic sport was slow in coming, dragging with it an age-old reluctance, even cynicism, about the place of females in the 'ring' – that enticing roped-off arena that has been dominated by men since it was first introduced by the Pugilistic Society in 1838.

Boxing itself has had a chequered reputation over the years, with serious concerns raised, among other things, about the safety of its participants. Part of the problem is a persistent confusion between the amateur and professional arms of the sport (no pun intended).

Born out of the ancient pastime of bare-knuckle 'prizefighting' – bare-fisted contests between two individuals, with spectators gambling on the outcome – boxing had no established regulations until 1867, when the Queensberry Rules formed the basis of the modern sport. Today, in both amateur and professional boxing, contestants tough it out in a ring, over 'rounds' or timed efforts of boxing, wearing padded gloves to minimise injury both to the boxer and to his/her opponent.

But there are essential distinctions between these two forms of the sport. In addition to differences in the judging and scoring systems, professional boxers wear no protective headgear, while amateurs are obliged to. Experienced professionals also box over many more rounds to win their championships – a fact which obviously incurs a greater risk of injury.

So while amateur and professional boxing are now strictly controlled by their respective governing bodies, and both enforce stringent safety standards, it is easy to understand why, for example, parents may yet entertain doubts about their youngsters' forays into the local boxing gym for sport and recreation.

Boxing fitness training will improve your clients' body composition, heart-lung stamina, strength, speed, coordination, balance and flexibility. It also has less tangible but equally important benefits, such as building discipline, confidence and self-esteem – especially relevant to schools and young people.

A HEALTHY SPORT

All this makes what Nicola Adams has done for *boxing* – not just women's boxing – even more significant. When she climbed into the ring, the picture of fitness, health and vitality, she became simultaneously a poster-person for boxing's physical benefits and a role model for its less tangible

ones. Her hard-knocks story (she worked on a building site to finance her training) gave her the drive to succeed against the odds, both inside and outside the ring. The Olympic Games were the forum for bringing that message, and its results, to a huge captive audience.

Nicola's Irish counterpart, and gold medallist in the lightweight division, Katie Taylor – who trained in a windowless former boathouse with no shower or toilet – fought equally hard behind the scenes, putting on exhibitions for the decision-makers as they determined whether women's boxing should be an Olympic sport. Katie's success in London brought a whole nation to a standstill as Ireland held its breath... unlike the roaring sea of green-clad supporters who witnessed her victory first-hand.

In reporting on the day's Olympic action, the media were correct in their assertion that, after all the hype, the *least* interesting aspect of Adams' and Taylor's performances was in fact their gender. What the two young women did was to cement a renewed public interest in the allure, skills and demands of amateur boxing – a sport now perfectly placed to touch the lives of even the most disadvantaged, hardest-to-reach young people.

A WIDESPREAD WORKOUT TREND

In the years leading up to the London Olympics, boxing was already regaining some of its former popularity, having become, in various non-contact forms, a widespread workout trend.

Health and fitness clubs introduced aerobics-type classes such as 'boxercise' and 'body combat' into their schedules, as clients discovered that routines incorporating boxing techniques and disciplines were both fun *and* highly effective in kick-starting their fitness gains.

Boxing gyms became less the exclusive domain of the macho man, and more a type of community venture – a place where people could feel a sense of belonging, while enjoying boxing-oriented social and sporting opportunities. And politicians, education experts and teachers caught on for the youngsters, too, with increasing numbers of schools incorporating non-contact boxing training into their timetables as a curricular or club activity.

As a fitness professional, all of the above represents huge opportunities for you. Boxing in its many forms is on the crest of a wave, and if you're a clued-up personal trainer, gym instructor or PE teacher, you'll want to get involved. *The Complete Guide to Boxing Fitness* shows you how.

WHAT IS BOXING FITNESS?

2

TRAINING 'OLD SCHOOL' – SAFELY

Out of the developments summarised in Chapter 1, there has grown a widespread awareness of the benefits of boxing fitness – which, in these pages, has a very specific definition.

> Boxing fitness comprises all the elements in a traditional boxer's training regime – but *without any glove-to-person contact.*

This does not mean boxing for wimps. It does mean training 'old school': shadow boxing, skipping, punching the heavy bag and hitting the focus pads – sweating it out just like a real boxer. But boxing fitness involves none of the potentially harmful contact made during sparring and competition, so that every session, properly undertaken, is guaranteed to be safe and injury-free for you and your clients.

Although you will be using this book to teach boxing fitness, you may find yourself approached by people wanting to try, for example, boxercise or kickboxing – these terms (and activities) still tend to get confused.

While boxing fitness can be taught in a group or class environment, as covered in Part Five of this book, it's not 'punching to music' and there is definitely no kicking involved. For your sake and your potential clients', be clear about what you do. When you have mastered the techniques and disciplines covered in these pages, you're a boxing trainer, and you teach technical boxing with all the attendant benefits – albeit without the element of contact.

> Boxing fitness uses shadow boxing, skipping, hitting the punch bag, glove-and-pad (focus pad) work, and core/abdominal training to shed the pounds, improve muscle tone, enhance heart-lung stamina and benefit performance in other sports and activities.

GOOD FOR YOUR CLIENTS – AND GOOD FOR YOU

For a number of reasons, boxing training – and glove-and-pad work in particular – can be an invaluable tool in your fitness armoury.

- It requires little equipment, so is flexible and low-cost for you and your pupils/clients.

- It can be done in a small indoor or outdoor space, with individuals or in a group/class setting.
- The training is both variable and intensive, achieving measurable results in a relatively short time span.
- Perhaps most importantly, it's fun. With the help of the ideas suggested in this book, and adding in your own, you can make each workout creative, progressive and enjoyable for everyone, yourself included.

However, while an increasing number of trainers and instructors are recognising these benefits and introducing boxing fitness to the general public, there are important considerations to bear in mind.

LEARN TO BOX!

Before you teach anyone else, you yourself need to learn the fundamentals of boxing. You don't need to be hugely skilled, and of course you don't need to compete. But without a solid theoretical and practical knowledge of the sport, you aren't in any position to teach it safely or effectively.

First, get to know the basics. Trainers who fail to wrap hands; who advise incorrectly on stance, punches and combinations; or who even stand by while one person, unqualified, holds the focus pads for another, are doing themselves and their clients no favours. Not only can such practices cause injury, they can also lead to boredom – a mental and physical 'plateau' for both pupil and teacher. The better a client's boxing skills, the more challenged and involved they become, and the more effectively you will be able to progress their training with increasingly complicated and satisfying drills and routines.

Then, you need to practise. To get the most out of your clients, the focus pads are an essential tool. And it's not really possible to do an effective glove-and-pad session if you, the trainer, have no idea how to box. For those who haven't held the pads before, when you turn to the relevant section of this book (Part Three) you'll see that it's far from a passive exercise, instead requiring you to duplicate a client's stance and actions and raise/lower the pads in response to the particular shots or combinations you require. This demands some measure of skill, and no little concentration – especially if the client works out of the opposite stance from you. The more familiar you are with the physical practice of boxing, the easier this becomes.

The Complete Guide to Boxing Fitness therefore provides you with a 'bible' of the principles and practices required both to learn and to teach tailor-made, safe and motivating boxing fitness programmes, at the same time enabling you to put an individual stamp on your training repertoire.

HOW TO USE THIS BOOK

The express aim of this book is to provide you with a comprehensive, practical resource for teaching non-contact boxing fitness to your pupils or clients. It is a boxing skills-based companion for those of you wishing to:

- Learn a new skill.
- Develop any existing expertise you may have in glove-and-pad (focus pad) work and other boxing training practices.
- Understand and apply the benefits of boxing fitness in a cross-training environment, helping others to improve their performance in a range of sporting disciplines.
- Where applicable, gain the necessary knowledge to 'train your trainers' – to teach

others the same skills, thus expanding and enhancing teamwork within your business or organisation.

As well as illustrated, step-by-step advice on how to impart core boxing and safety techniques to your clients, you will also find in these pages:

• Useful contributions and quotes from a range of practitioners, including boxing coaches, personal trainers, schools' PE teachers and other sports instructors, together with feed-back from their clients/students/pupils.
• Up-to-date and relevant information on health and safety and other legislative requirements for delivering boxing training, together with options for Continuing Professional Development and current developments in the boxing and fitness industry arenas.
• A range of creative boxing-related drills and skills, devised by the author, contributors and other coaches, and tailored to different train-ing systems, as well as cross-training for other sports (e.g. specific drills to develop strength, endurance, speed, cardiovascular fitness, isometric and core stability).

• Sample training programmes for clients of differing abilities and fitness levels, with guidance on safe and appropriate progression.
• A glossary of boxing terminology with further references and resources for the fitness professional.
• Relevant content on injury prevention and treatment, and dietary and health matters.

Ideally you will cover all the sections in turn, so that you fully understand each individual element in boxing fitness – why do it, how to do it, and how to teach it – as well as acquiring a holistic view of the way in which the sessions build and fit together. But of course, depending on your level of boxing knowledge and experience, you may wish to dip in and out of the most relevant parts: the book is structured clearly to help you navigate with ease.

And a final word: once you're familiar and confi-dent with the basics, don't be afraid to introduce your own innovations. One of the beauties of this type of training is its potential for creativity; use yours, and your sessions need never grow stale. To use that phrase much-loved by seasoned boxing trainers, 'Box clever!' If you do, you'll find that your services as an exercise professional are always in demand.

PART **ONE**

HANDS UP!
ESSENTIAL PREPARATION
FOR YOU AND YOUR CLIENTS

LEGISLATIVE AND PROFESSIONAL REQUIREMENTS

3

FOR PE TEACHERS

If you're a qualified PE teacher employed by a school, you will already have undergone the necessary criminal records (CRB) check in order to work with young people; you should also possess a current first aid qualification or have a qualified first-aider on site. There are few health and safety risks associated with non-contact boxing fitness, especially if you follow the basic precautions outlined in this book. However, it is advisable to contact the insurance company and check that you and your school are fully covered for this type of training.

It's possible that your insurers and/or employer may require you to hold a formal boxing qualification – perhaps one that is endorsed by the national sports governing body. In the UK, the GB National Boxing Awards (www.boxing awards.co.uk/index.php) offer an ideal solution.

Run in association with the Amateur Boxing Association (ABA, www.abae.co.uk) and other key partners, the Awards are broken down into six levels. The first three (Preliminary, Standard and Bronze) are non-contact, cover the basics of boxing, and will give you a Boxing Tutor qualification* – enabling you to teach in any non-specialist facility such as your school hall or gymnasium. Courses are held regularly in a range of locations: more information is available from the website and included in the 'Further resources' section at the end of this book.

Outside the UK, try getting in touch with the local branch of your national amateur boxing federation – contact details are available from the International Boxing Association (AIBA, www.aiba.org) – to enquire what equivalent qualifications may be available to you, and how to access them.

FOR PERSONAL TRAINERS AND FITNESS INSTRUCTORS

In addition to your professional personal training diploma or equivalent, you will need to ensure that your public liability insurance is adequate and

---

* If you so wish, for your own Continuing Professional Development you can progress through the Boxing Awards to the Silver, Gold and Platinum standards. These involve technique development via semi-contact or full-contact sparring, and so can only be undertaken in a boxing club under the supervision of a qualified ABA Coach. Students can also participate in the GB National Boxing Awards, which give them credits towards the ABA National Boxing Educational Qualification.

up-to-date to cover non-contact boxing training with clients – wherever you intend to train them.

If you are a gym instructor, legal requirements may vary depending on whether you are employed by your organisation or self-employed and 'renting' space. Speak to the appropriate person in charge and let them know you're intending to start boxing fitness with a client or group/class. In the unlikely event that they are not familiar with boxing training, emphasise that it is non-contact and take along a copy of this book for them to look through. Once they see what's involved, they should be able to advise whether you require any additional insurance or other type of cover before beginning (see also Chapter 4, 'Essential equipment').

FOR COACHES IN OTHER SPORTS

As well as the above, stress to your organisation and athletes – and parents or carers if appropriate – that boxing is an excellent form of cross-training, enhancing strength, speed, stamina, balance, coordination and focus to the benefit of performance in a range of activities and disciplines. Part

Five of this *Complete Guide* is especially relevant to you.

Once you have worked through all the sections in this book, you will be well prepared to teach boxing fitness safely and effectively. However, you may also wish to hold a formal qualification, in boxing generally or in glove-and-pad (focus pad) work specifically. As well as the Boxing Awards mentioned above, which are open to personal trainers and other exercise professionals, you could attend a specialist course to build on your technical knowledge and practical experience.

You'll find that a number of local, national and international organisations now offer such courses, and most advertise on the internet; alternatively you could ask the training provider with whom you originally gained your qualification. Do your research, and make sure any boxing training course you choose is accredited by a recognised fitness industry body and, preferably, carries Continuing Professional Development (CPD) points. Some suggestions are included in the 'Further resources' section.

ORGANISING YOUR TRAINING SESSIONS

4

Once confident that you are fully covered both legally and professionally, it's time to turn your mind to organising your training sessions.

VENUE

Look at the venue(s) available to you. You may be using a park or other outdoor space; a fitness centre, gymnasium or sports hall; or, if you're a mobile personal trainer, somebody's home or garden. Any and all of these are suitable for boxing fitness if you bear in mind a few key points.

Depending on which combination of boxing disciplines you're intending to teach, make sure there is sufficient room for you and your client(s) to move around freely with no potential slip or trip hazards. Eliminate any of the usual health and safety suspects such as stray wires, errant pets and loose rugs or other items indoors, and hidden tree roots or large stones outdoors. The floor should be level and ideally neither too hard – concrete and other unyielding surfaces can lead to lower-limb soreness and even shin splints when skipping – nor too soft – soggy ground or thick, plush carpets make footwork difficult and can risk the client stumbling.

If you are working one-on-one or two-on-one, you can do so effectively in a few square metres of space. You just need sufficient room to move around during shadow boxing and glove-and-pad work, and for skipping (if you are indoors, remember to check the ceiling height and the positioning of any light or decorative fixtures). For a group or class you will need an equivalent amount of space around each individual or pair of participants.

ESSENTIAL EQUIPMENT

The following personal equipment is essential for teaching boxing fitness effectively.

For the client:
- a pair of **hand-wraps**;
- a pair of **boxing gloves**;
- a **skipping rope**.

For you:
- a pair of professional-standard **focus pads** (also called focus mitts);
- a **method of timing rounds**.

HAND-WRAPS

Hand-wraps are worn inside the boxing glove for several reasons, the most important being injury prevention.

It's commonly believed that wraps protect the knuckles, but in fact this part of the hand is strong and unlikely to suffer injury apart from potentially some superficial abrasions (see Part Four for some common, minor boxing-related ailments and their prevention/treatment). Instead it is the small bones in the hands and wrists that may be hurt if an inexperienced practitioner makes contact with the punch bag or focus pads incorrectly. The hand-wraps therefore act as a support as well as 'filling up' any space inside the glove, so that the client can form a solid, protected fist to punch with.

Additionally, unlike leather boxing gloves, hand-wraps can be washed regularly. If you're

Wrapping your clients' hands is not optional; it is a requirement of safe boxing practice.

teaching it well, boxing fitness will make your client (and you) sweat: it's therefore good hygiene to ensure that they have a pair of clean wraps to wear for each session.

Ideally you will advise them to purchase their own hand-wraps, which can be done cheaply on the internet or at most good sports shops (some recommendations are included in the 'Further resources' section). 'Mexican' style hand-wraps are a good choice, as they're more stretchy than cotton and

therefore mould to the hand for a good fit. Adidas makes its AIBA-approved wraps in 255cm and 450cm lengths, for smaller and larger hands (these are the minimum and maximum lengths respectively for a competitive amateur boxing bout).

For people just starting out or having a trial session, it's a good idea to carry a couple of spare, clean pairs of hand-wraps in your gym bag at all times.

If you are working with groups or classes, for example at a health club or school, obviously it is more difficult to ask each participant to provide their own wraps. Stress the important function of hand-wraps to your organisation, and request that they invest in a sufficient number of pairs to cover your maximum attendance. Make sure these are returned after each class and are laundered regularly.

The technique for hand-wrapping is covered in Chapter 5, together with some tips on managing this effectively in a busy group environment.

BOXING GLOVES

There are two types of glove available for boxing training: bag gloves, or mitts (shown bottom right), and sparring gloves (top right). Bag gloves are lightly cushioned 'slip-on' gloves designed to be worn over wraps to protect the hands when in contact with the punch bag or focus pads.

Sparring gloves are more substantially padded and come in different sizes expressed by weight: the smallest are usually 10oz and the largest 16oz. They fasten firmly around the wrist area, with Velcro or sometimes still with laces, and the thumb is stitched to the body of the glove rather than being 'loose' or even open, as with bag gloves.

Sparring gloves are traditionally worn for boxing training that involves contact with another

person – i.e. sparring, or mock contests between two individuals for technical development and conditioning purposes. Having said this, although boxing fitness is non-contact, it is generally wise to start your clients off in sparring gloves rather than bag gloves – at least until they have practised and are familiar with the correct punching techniques. With beginners wearing light bag gloves there is a chance of awkward contact with the focus pads, resulting in sore thumbs, hands or wrists.

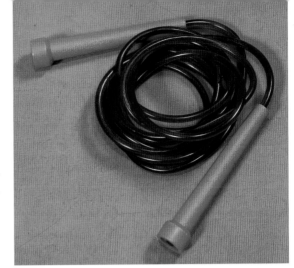

As with hand-wraps, in an ideal world each of your clients or pupils would own their own boxing gloves. But while a pair of wraps is a relatively small expense, sparring gloves can be a costly outlay. As an exercise professional it will stand you in good stead to purchase a small number of good-quality leather sparring gloves in a range of sizes, for your clients to borrow. Air them out after each session.

If you are affiliated to an organisation, check out the 'Further resources' section for manufacturer recommendations and pass these along to whoever is in charge of ordering equipment, together with the manufacturers' contact details. Buying in bulk will usually get you a discount: don't hesitate to ask. And for groups or classes, you don't necessarily need to have one pair of gloves per participant; one between two can suffice (see Part Five on organising boxing fitness in a class environment).

SKIPPING ROPES

Skipping is a fundamental part of boxing training. Not only does it build endurance, challenging the heart, lungs and muscles, it also develops balance, coordination and agility. Boxing requires all these skills for the effective delivery of punches and combinations, and for dextrous footwork.

For your clients, a light plastic 'speed rope' (above right) is the best choice. These are inexpensive, weigh almost nothing for you to carry around, and are easily purchased over the internet or from most decent sports shops. If you are working with a large group or class, consider removing the handles from the speed ropes: participants can simply hold the ends of the plastic and still skip effectively, but if someone else gets hit – and skipping ropes *can* fly around, even with the most

careful monitoring – it doesn't hurt. This is especially useful with younger kids in schools!

FOCUS PADS

Your focus pads (above) – also called focus mitts or hook-and-jab pads – are the professional tools of your trade. Invest in a quality pair that suits your requirements and those of your clients, and for safety purposes never lend them to anyone else to have a go; you can't assume they know how to use them properly.

The focus pad comprises a glove into which you slip your fingers, usually secured at the wrist with a Velcro strip. The front part of the glove is approximately 7.5cm of shock-dispersing, aerated foam padding designed to absorb a boxer's punches, resulting in reduced impact on your hands and wrists (and by extension your arms and shoulders). Some pads feature a finger guard to protect the ends of your fingers against stray shots.

Beyond these basic features, focus pad design varies, and you should try before you buy in order to find out which pads suit you best. Some have a larger surface area suitable for novice clients who might not be able to target their punches accurately. Others are extra-padded for heavy hitters. Some are curved for comfortable hand positioning and incorporate a 'grip ball' to aid secure handling: there are trainers who feel that flat pads enable them to better feel the accuracy of a client's punches and assess their balance.

Prices vary considerably too, and usually in direct correlation to quality. Don't skimp on your investment, and whichever kind of pads you choose, keep an eye on them to see when they need replacing. Repeated punches over time will flatten out the padding, potentially increasing impact and thus wear and tear on your joints.

A METHOD OF TIMING ROUNDS

Both amateur and professional contests are measured in rounds – regular intervals of boxing. For the professionals, a round usually lasts three minutes; for amateurs, depending on age and experience, boxers may compete over one-and-a-half, two or three minutes. The total number of rounds in a bout also varies. What doesn't vary, ever, is the rest period between rounds, which is always 60 seconds.

Because of this competition structure, boxers organise their training around the same intervals, and therefore need a way of measuring rounds

during workouts. To teach your clients, you require the same.

It's unlikely, but you may be working where there is a traditional boxing clock (see above). This has a single electronic hand to denote the passing of each minute: a bell denotes the start and end of the rest period. Such clocks make many an old pro nostalgic, but are rarely seen these days due to cost and the need for wiring-in. More affordable and convenient variations are now available, such as the Gymboss Interval Timer (www.gymboss. com), which costs less than a decent stopwatch. If you're working at someone's house or in a gym, see if you can keep an eye on a normal wall clock that has a second hand.

Bear in mind that your smartphone, watch or stopwatch is not ideal for this purpose. You may find yourself fiddling with it and thus not focusing sufficiently on your client; it's also well-nigh impossible to check the passage of rounds on one when you're holding the focus pads.

OTHER BOXING FITNESS EQUIPMENT

The equipment listed above is the minimum required to teach an effective, results-based boxing fitness session. With these portable, easily purchased and inexpensive tools, together with this book and your creative brain, the world is your virtual boxing ring and clients will keep on stepping through its ropes.

However, if you wish to and are able to access the facilities, you may also incorporate punch bag and speed ball work into your programme. Add in an *actual* boxing ring, and you have the perfect boxing fitness environment.

PUNCH BAG

Also commonly known as the heavy bag, your clients can hit this to practise a broad repertoire of punches and combinations, as well as to improve their footwork and defence techniques. Bag work is hard cardiovascular training, ideal for achieving general weight loss and toning; you can structure sessions variously to build muscular endurance, strength, power and stamina (see Part Two for specific teaching suggestions).

There are a number of types of punch bag available, each fulfilling a slightly different function. All are made of leather or a tough synthetic material filled with padding to provide a cushioned resistance to shots. They can be cylindrical (see right); 'angle-cut' to allow punches from a range of directions; or hung higher with a flat base for practising uppercuts. They can be suspended on chains from ceiling joists, wall-mounted on special brackets, or free-standing.

You may be fortunate enough to teach in a venue that already has ceiling- or wall-mounted punch bags. Alternatively, you could buy, or ask your organisation to purchase, a free-standing bag that can be moved out of the way and stored when not in use. Choose a type that is not too fixed or rigid when punched: with good reciprocal movement in the bag, your students can work effectively on reaction times, balanced footwork, defences and lateral (evasive) head movement.

SPEED BALL (see top right)

This is a small, air-filled bag anchored to a 'rebound platform' that is mounted parallel to the ground. Working on the speed ball improves speed and hand-eye coordination. It is a useful add-on to a basic boxing session, but is not essential, and unless you are teaching in a specialised boxing club or gym it's unlikely that you will have access to one.

BOXING RING (bottom right)

As with the boxing clock above, let's include a mention of this authentic, alluring bit of boxing tradition. The modern boxing ring is set on a raised platform of between 4.9m and 6.1m square feet, covered with padding and a durable canvas. There is a post at each corner of the ring, to which are fixed four parallel rows of ropes that form a flexible, continuous barrier enclosing the boxing arena. The ropes are further secured by vertical strips, holding them together and thus reducing the risk of anyone falling through them to the floor below.

It's hard to describe the feeling when you step into a boxing ring, but there is something quite special about it – even if you're not about to compete. Try to experience it for yourself and, if possible, see if you can find a ring for your clients to work out in; they're bound to find it exciting. They may also note that the particular combination of sprung boards, padding and non-slip ring canvas promotes grip for improved delivery of punches and combinations, as well as aiding their footwork.

If you're looking for venues with boxing rings, do your research creatively. As well as the obvious, like traditional boxing clubs or gyms in your area, you could try facilities where they teach other fight disciplines such as kickboxing, Mixed Martial Arts (MMA), Thai boxing or Jujitsu. Some of the

larger and wealthier health clubs are starting to feature a training ring, having recognised the 'pull' this can exert on their clients.

CARDIO, WEIGHTS AND OTHER TRAINING EQUIPMENT/AIDS

Boxing fitness can be further augmented and varied with the creative use of other equipment, such as free- or machine-weights, cardio aids such as step machines, rowers and treadmills, and Swiss and medicine balls. If you have access to such things, you'll need to use your professional judgement and creative mind as to whether/how

It's a good idea to build a client's cardio work around intervals comprising hard one-and-a-half, two- or three-minute efforts with one minute's recovery. This simulates the rest traditionally taken by boxers between competitive rounds, with the effect of training the heart, lungs and muscles to recover quickly and efficiently over a brief, set period. Seeing to what extent their heart rate returns to near-normal during the 60 seconds can be a good indication of progress made or needed.

you choose to incorporate them into a boxing programme. Although it is not within the remit of this book to cover such training add-ons in any detail, Part Five includes a few tried-and-tested combinations, as well as some old-school boxing tricks you might find useful and fun to try.

For inexperienced or unfit clients, in the early days it's unrealistic to plan a full hour of shadow boxing, punch bag or focus pad work and skipping; boxing training is intensive. In such cases it can be good to use light weights. If you're working at their house or in the park, you might take some along with you – and/or incorporate circuit and Swiss ball core work, giving you other options for a full and varied session without making them feel low about their fitness levels.

ESTABLISHING YOUR CLIENTS'/PUPILS' GOALS

At the risk of teaching grannies to suck eggs, before starting out you will need to establish your clients' goals and aspirations. As you've already learnt, this is essential for exercise professionals working in any area of the fitness industry. To ensure client retention – and therefore safeguard your income and reputation – your sessions and programmes need to be safe, fun and creative; they also need to be effective. This can only be achieved if they work *for* the client, and are tailor-made to meet individual needs.

Of course, this may be more relevant to personal trainers and gym instructors than, say, to school PE teachers who have a mixed-ability class to teach. Even for the latter, however, it's important to be clear about your aims (which are, or should be, the same as theirs – even if they don't know it!). You may be looking to improve pupils' general health and fitness through exercise, in which case

boxing training is as good as, if not better than, many other types of physical activity. Or you may need to consider how best to use boxing fitness in a cross-training capacity, to improve students' performance in other sports.

The point is to think about it carefully. As just one example, consider a group of young people whose focus is on football. Which necessary skills might be enhanced through boxing training? Working on footwork will aid their balance and agility on the pitch. Skipping will do the same, with the added bonus of increasing stamina. Boxing is comprised of interval-based work, and so is football – bursts of hard effort with the ball, or to get into position to receive and pass it, with brief periods of recovery; so boxing over set rounds and rest periods can help footballers recover between sprints much more efficiently.

It's your job to ask the right questions, and do the right assessments, to find out what your clients or pupils really want to achieve. Many people will just say, 'I want to be fitter' or 'I want to lose weight' – but what do they *actually* mean? Get to the heart of it. It's likely that your clients won't know how the word 'fitness' tends to be used as a catch-all, encompassing all the different (usually physical) qualities that we can improve and enhance through exercise. Use your knowledge and experience to tease out whether they want to improve their heart/lung efficiency, muscular endurance, strength, speed, power, body composition, or joint range of motion; or a combination of these things. In this way you'll be able to tailor your sessions and programmes in order to get the best results.

Here's a brief recap of the main components of physical fitness, as defined by the American College of Sports Medicine:

1. Cardiovascular (also called aerobic) fitness – capacity of the heart, lungs, and blood-carrying vessels to deliver oxygen; referring to the efficient working of the heart, lungs and circulatory system.
2. Muscular endurance – the ability of a muscle or group of muscles to perform repeated contractions or hold static contractions.
3. Muscular strength – the amount of force a muscle or group of muscles can exert in a single all-out effort, usually against some kind of resistance.
4. Flexibility – refers to a joint's range of motion (ROM).
5. Body composition – the ratio of lean body mass (muscle, bone, tendons and ligaments) to fat mass.

Also consider:
1. Speed – how fast a movement or series of movements can be performed.
2. Power – comprising both muscular strength and speed together.

Remember that while benefiting from any or all of these fitness gains, your client's main motivation for exercise may not be physical at all. They may simply wish to find a healthy, therapeutic outlet for the stress of their everyday life.

Finally, when establishing and setting goals with your clients, always be realistic. Boxing fitness is surprisingly hard work: the last thing you want is to hit your client (figuratively) with too much too soon, so they lose confidence and give up. Nor do you want to make it too easy, or they won't be motivated. Judging this is one of the beauties and the challenges of your job!

One great thing about boxing training is that it's highly flexible. If a client is coasting, you can

'I have to box now. I started boxing fitness a couple of years ago and have benefited in so many ways. I have a very demanding job that creates a lot of stress. No other form of exercise makes me feel quite so relaxed and able to deal with the pressures and frustrations of my job. After an hour boxing and punching the focus pads my stress levels are right down and the difficult day I've had is forgotten. It has increased my strength and stamina and I really look forward to it each week. If people of any age or ability want to get fitter and stronger, I can't think of a better form of exercise.'
(Female SEN Teacher, 50)

use *overload* – getting them to punch harder and/or faster, over longer periods or with less rest – to increase the intensity of their efforts. And vice versa for a pupil who may be struggling. If they are easily bored, when you've read this book and come up with your own ideas you will have plenty of new drills and skills to introduce. There is really no excuse for your sessions to become stale.

Remember to keep a record of any specific aims that you and your clients establish together, and be sure to monitor their progress regularly, preferably in written form, so you have something to show them by which they can concretely measure and enjoy their progress.

You are probably already using your own, branded client assessment documents, but for useful reference, templates for the following documents are included as an Appendix to this book: Client/Trainer Agreement; Short- and Long-Term Client Goals; Client Food Diary; Physical Activity Readiness Questionnaire (PAR-Q).

PREPARING PROPERLY – AND // WRAPPING HANDS

5

Before you start any training session, go over all the basics. This is both a physical and a mental process.

WHAT DO YOU NEED?

Do you have – or have access to – all the equipment you need for the session you've planned? Within reason, cater for the unforeseen, such as an extra person turning up to your class or someone forgetting their hand-wraps. Carry a few spares with you when possible. Don't forget your interval timer if there isn't a suitable clock at the venue, and it may sound obvious, but check that

'I once turned up to a group session with only one focus pad. What I had thought was the other one was in fact a similar-coloured sparring glove. Thinking on my feet, I pretended that I meant to work with only one pad – by chance, discovering that getting clients to perform standard combinations "across their body" on a smaller, narrower target really works the core. I now use single-pad work in a lot of sessions, but it was a nasty moment.' (Personal trainer/boxing fitness instructor)

any gloves you're providing are in matched pairs and that you have both of your focus pads.

As well as making your mental equipment-check, ensure that you look after yourself. Take plenty of water, a towel, and a spare dry top to every session. You may sweat a lot: as you'll discover, boxing fitness is interactive for the trainer as well as being intensive for the clients/pupils. Put cool/warm/wet weather gear in your gym bag to suit the conditions.

This isn't facile advice. It's all too common for an instructor to neglect themselves in the process of looking after their clients. You're not doing anyone any favours if you work when over-tired, ill or injured. Check in with yourself regularly, to see how your body and mind are holding up. If you don't feel great, reduce the amount of physical work you do within the session or postpone it altogether. Of course you need the money and you don't want to let people down. But better to disappoint them once in order to rest and get yourself back on track than to drag it out and risk a prolonged absence or injury.

WHAT DO THEY NEED?

During their initial consultation you will have advised your client(s) what to bring and wear to their boxing sessions. Boxing fitness doesn't require any special kit or shoes; sensible workout gear and a good-quality pair of supportive trainers are perfectly adequate. Several thin layers of clothing are recommended, since these can be gradually shed as the client warms up, and put back on for the cool-down. Because boxing is an intensive form of exercise, there will be a lot of sweating – if you're teaching it right! The body chills very quickly as moisture evaporates from the skin, so it's important for your clients to get warm and dry as soon as their workout is over. For the same reason, they should always have access to fresh water for rehydration, and a clean dry towel.

We have already talked about hand-wraps, skipping ropes and gloves. When your clients are fairly experienced, there is an argument for suggesting that they also invest in a pair of boxing boots. Some of the techniques you will be teaching involve agile footwork, with quite a lot of lateral movement in the lower limb. Training shoes tend not to support this area effectively, whereas boxing boots lace higher up the shin – sometimes even to knee level – to provide stability and protection. They are 'breathable', allowing for the air to circulate and preventing sweat build-up; and they have rubber grip soles, giving firm traction. Boxing boots don't have to cost the earth; a reasonable pair can be bought for around half the price of a pair of specialist running shoes. You may wish to consider buying a pair yourself.

HEALTH CHECKS

Before you begin the session, and once you have done your venue health and safety checks, confirm that your clients or pupils are fit to exercise. In the case of minor complaints and injuries, you'll have to use your judgement as to whether they can participate in all or part of the workout (see Part Four for some common boxing-related ailments and how to treat or prevent them).

It's not advisable for anyone to work out when suffering from a virus such as a cold, even if they are keen to do so and have signed a disclaimer as part of their Physical Activity Readiness Questionnaire (PAR-Q) at the client consultation stage (see Appendix). Explain that exercise can worsen their condition; advise bed rest with plenty of fluids and, if applicable, over-the-counter remedies. If their health doesn't quickly improve, you should recommend that they consult their doctor.

THE WARM-UP

Once you've established that everyone is good to go, start the warm-up. You're an exercise professional, so will already know the importance of this. For boxing training, make sure you include some general mobility exercises followed by a good pulse-raiser, a full set of dynamic or static stretches, and another quick pulse-raiser. This will increase blood circulation to raise both the general body and deep muscle temperatures, in turn helping to prepare muscles, ligaments and tendons for the more vigorous activity to follow.

Plenty of clients would skip the warm-up if they could. A common cry is, 'But I just want to start boxing.' Explain briefly that boxing involves high-intensity exercise efforts and, in addition, may use muscles they didn't know they had. A good warm-up will reduce the likelihood of injury and post-exercise soreness, while improving athletic performance, muscle efficiency, reaction time and speed of movement. In other words, make it an essential part of the session.

The warm-up should last around 10–15 minutes, depending on what type of activity will follow immediately afterwards. If you intend to go straight into hard focus pad work, it should be very thorough – raising a sweat and really lubricating the joints. If shadow boxing and skipping will come first, these activities will act to further warm the muscles and raise the heart rate, so the warm-up could be a little briefer.

Take into account the ambient temperature. If you're working in a park on a cold winter evening, obviously the active warm-up should be longer and more intensive than in a heated gym or sports hall, or outside on a sunny day. But always remember that the warm-up is about raising the deep body temperature – not just wearing lots of clothing. Stinting on it is never a good idea.

Don't fall into the trap of thinking that boxing is all focused on the arms and hands. It involves every part of the body and particularly the shoulders, upper back, core, hips, knees and ankles. This will become clearer when we have discussed the various techniques; for the moment, note that it's essential to do a full-body warm up without neglecting any muscles or joints.

MAKE IT RELEVANT – AND FUN

Consider ways in which you can incorporate boxing-related activities into the standard warm-up to make it more interesting and appropriate for the session to follow. For example, you could have your client jogging on the spot or round a small circuit, punching out in front of them, up in the air, down towards the ground and to their sides – always making sure there is enough space so they don't whack someone by accident. They'll find it surprisingly hard work.

In a group situation – or with an individual client, with you as the other partner – you could try pairing people up, facing each other in the boxing *stance* (see Chapter 7). One partner is A, and the other is B. Over a set time period – perhaps a minute – A uses their jab (lead) hand to try to touch B's body; it is B's job to get out of the way. At the end of the minute they swap roles. Alternatively A uses their front foot to try to touch B's; B must move their feet quickly to get away. After a minute, swap roles. Depending on the situation you could set forfeits: for example, every time B is tagged they do five press-ups or tuck-jumps. This is sure to keep them focused and engaged.

Encourage both partners to treat these drills as a serious boxing warm-up, *not* a brawl or a foot-stamping exercise. They should remain in their stance with their guard up, using foot, body and head movement to keep ahead of the game. It's all about reflexes – getting the mind, heart, lungs and muscles ready for the session ahead. And it's about having fun. Some more suggestions for partner drills are included in Chapter 12: try them, and think up your own.

WRAPPING THE HANDS

Some boxing instructors wrap their client's hands before they do anything else – even prior to starting the general warm-up, when it's not strictly necessary (as the client's hands won't yet be making contact with anything).

There is a good argument for doing this. Often, clients or pupils are keen to try out the boxing equipment and especially to put on gloves, as soon as they arrive at the training venue. They want to see what it *feels* like to be a boxer. It may sound silly, but if you wrap their hands immediately on entering, they somehow feel more 'professional' and focused on their session. It will also help to get them used to keeping their hands in the correct position as they make a fist, in preparation for wearing the gloves.

When you read the hand-wrapping instructions given below, you'll realise that it's quite a time-consuming process, especially when you're not used to doing it. If you have just one student, no problem – but if you have a class, wrapping each person's hands can use up a lot of the session.

One idea for getting around this is to spend part of your group's introductory workout explaining and demonstrating how they can do their own wraps. If they know that this slightly onerous exercise will avoid eating into their precious boxing time in the future, they'll understand and be happy to have a try. You can go around the class checking their technique, advising, and assisting where necessary. Alternatively, pair people up and get them to do each other's hands.

The only way to learn hand-wrapping technique is to practise: on yourself and on other people. It's common to be able to do one of your own hands trouble-free and to struggle with the other for a while, but the whole thing does get easier.

The description below is for you wrapping a client's hands, rather than your own. In terms of method, there are many variations and preferences, but the important thing is to find a way that is safe, quick and effective. The *Do's and Don'ts* at the end of this section provide a useful checklist.

- You can either start with the hand-wrap rolled up, or unrolled. If rolled, make sure it has been done beginning with the Velcro end and finishing with the thumb-loop at the outside. (Hand-wraps do have a top and

a bottom; some are even marked 'This Side Down' because you need the Velcro to be face-up when you've finished. If you find you started with the wrong side down, you don't need to begin all over again. On the last turn around the wrist, simply flip or twist the hand-wrap over and you can then fasten the Velcro securely.) If you start with the wrap unrolled, make sure it doesn't get tangled or caught in anything; the Velcro is – obviously – sticky.

- Ask your client to hold one hand out flat, palm down and fingers slightly spread in a relaxed way. Then put the thumb-loop around the thumb. Wrap the fabric around their wrist several times, moving up their forearm towards the elbow a good 5–7.5cm to ensure that the wrist is well protected (see figure 5.1a). Make sure that the wrap is firm, secure and smooth around the wrist but *not too tight* – you don't want to inhibit their circulation. To check, slip the ends of your fingers underneath the edges, and ask them for feedback.

- Moving back towards their hand, wrap across the top of the hand and around the knuckles 2–3 times (see figure 5.1b). Ask them to keep their fingers slightly spread. The hand-wrap should form a cushion over the knuckles and extend just slightly over the ends of the fingers as they join the hand (but not as far as the first joint). Make sure your client can close and open their fist a couple of times, and wiggle their fingers: it's important that they can still do this comfortably.

- Bring the hand-wrap back around the wrist and wrap this again at least one full time. Then bring the wrap under the wrist and over the base of the thumb (see figures 5.1c and d). Wind the fabric around the thumb and back

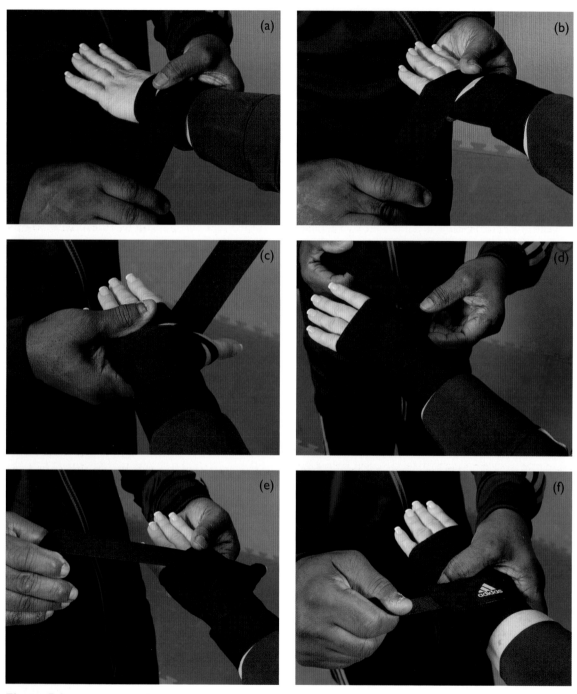

Figure 5.1

over the top of the hand. *You are aiming to cover all the areas of skin that are visible* – literally 'wrapping' their hand like a parcel, so that none of it is exposed.

- Pass the wrap around the knuckles once more, then do figure-of-eights – crossing over the back of their hand, around their wrist, back over the hand, around the knuckles (see figure 5.1e).
- As you start to run out of material, make sure that you finish at the wrist. Wrap around the wrist one final time and secure the hand-wrap with the Velcro strip (see figure 5.1f).

Especially towards the start of their boxing training, your clients' knuckles may get a little sore and chafed. This is particularly so with punch bag work. In such cases try cutting an ordinary bath sponge in half and placing one half on each hand, over the knuckles. Then wrap the hands as normal, over the top of the sponge. The client can help you by holding the sponge in place until it is securely covered by the wrap.

CHECKLIST FOR SAFE AND EFFECTIVE HAND-WRAPPING

Do:

- Make sure your client spreads their fingers while you are wrapping, to ensure that the hand-wrap is not too tight.

- Start and finish wrapping at the wrist – good wrist support is essential to avoid injury.
- Make sure that the whole hand is covered, the thumb securely wrapped, and a cushion of material lies over the knuckles.
- Check that during the process, and at the end, they can still wiggle their fingers and make a fist comfortably; the wrap should not feel constrictive or cause discomfort at any time.

Don't:

- Use wraps that are still wet with sweat from a previous session: as well as being unhygienic, this can cause blisters. After work, if you're not going to launder the wraps, hang them out unrolled on a radiator or line.
- Use really long wraps on tiny hands, or short wraps on big hands. The former will bunch up and slip around beneath the boxing glove; the latter won't provide enough cushioning or support.
- Wind the wraps between the fingers unless the client specifically wants this. Some boxers use this technique but it can cause chafing between the digits and even inflammation of the knuckle joints.

When everyone's hands are wrapped – either pre- or post-warm-up – you are ready to teach the individual boxing fitness disciplines. These are covered in the following section.

2

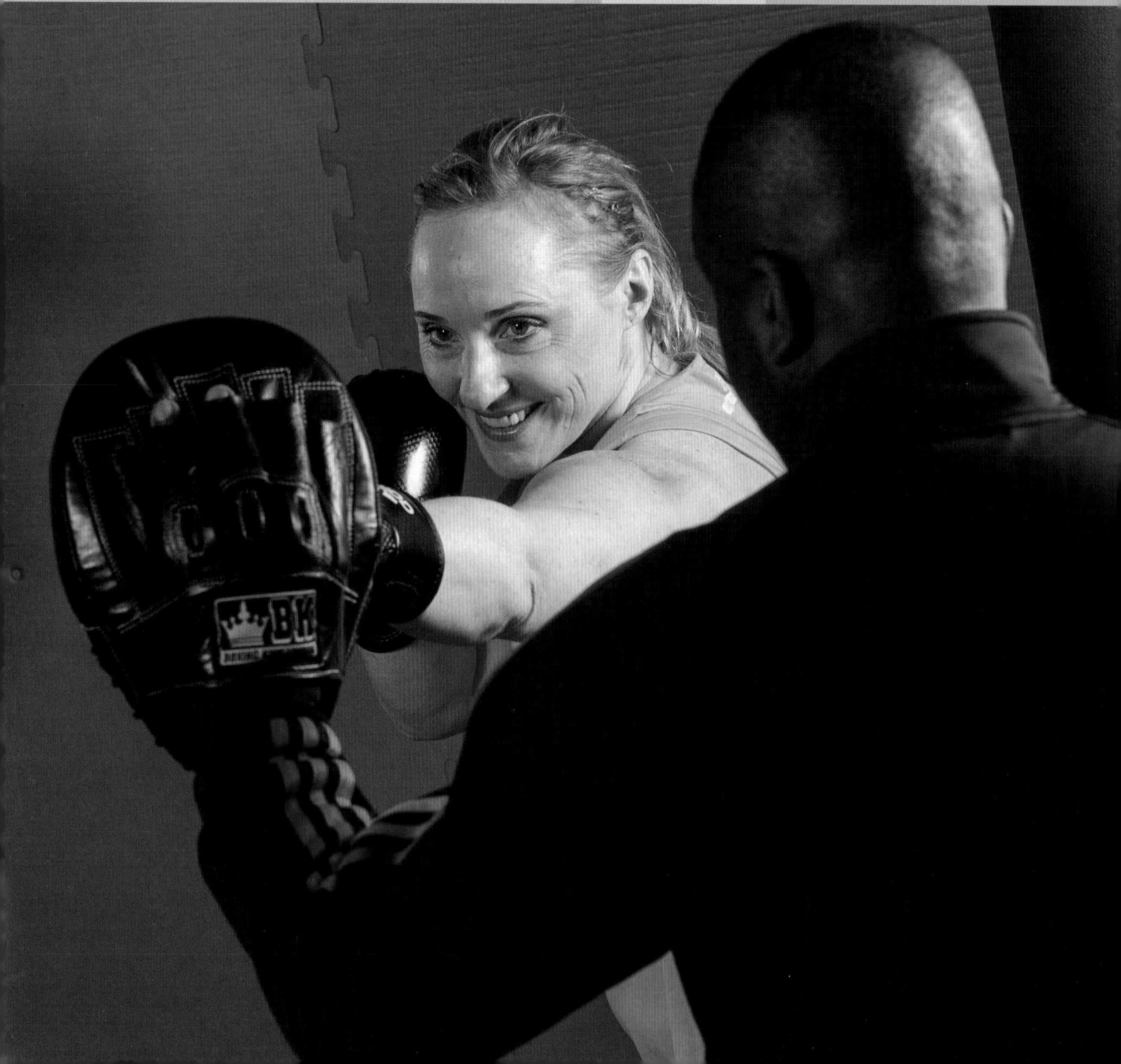

PART **TWO**

TEACHING THE CORE TECHNIQUES

THE IMPORTANCE OF CORRECT TECHNIQUE

6

As previous chapters should have made clear, it is essential that you learn and teach the correct basic boxing techniques from the outset. Some exercise professionals think that because their clients or pupils are unlikely ever to climb through the ropes of a boxing ring to make contact with another person, it doesn't matter how they punch. In fact, nothing could be further from the truth.

It *is* true that for the purposes of improving someone's fitness, you don't need to learn or teach pure technical boxing to the level of an amateur (or a professional) competitor. But neither can you just instruct a client to 'hit the bag' or 'hit the focus pad'.

Take someone who is aiming a straight punch – a jab or a cross/back hand (see pages 43–9 for step-by-step instructions). If, instead of keeping the elbow of the active arm close to the body, aiming the punch directly out from the shoulder, they raise the elbow laterally, this changes the angle of the striking hand.

Try it yourself, now. Instead of the knuckled part of the fist making the desired, strong and straight contact with the bag or mitt, it will be the outside of the hand near the knuckle of the little finger. This has the effect of shortening and weakening the punch, which may not matter for the sake of fitness, but repeated over time risks bruising at best, and injury at worst. And the injury may not be simply to the little-finger knuckle joint, but possibly of an additional, compensatory nature to other parts of the body such as the wrist or shoulder.

This is not meant to scare you (or your clients!). Of course your clients will make mistakes: no one gets the techniques perfect all the time. But from your point of view you need to know the risks in order to keep a careful eye on their progress and prevent any bad habits from setting in too fixedly. Learning the punches and combinations takes time and practice as you and your students build 'muscle memory' and the movements become second nature. This is a great development, because it enables you both to try and enjoy increasingly complicated drills and routines that keep the challenge fresh and the positive fitness adaptations coming. But if the 'muscle memory' is of poor, potentially harmful punching technique, it will be much harder to iron out these kinks when they start causing problems later on.

The same is true of your own focus pad technique. Holding the pads is a skill in itself, not a passive exercise, and you need to take the time to develop this skill correctly from the outset. A common fault is to 'slap' with the pads – pushing them out with force to meet the client's gloves as they punch; this can be overwhelming and even scary for them, as well as potentially causing soreness or injury in both parties. But neither do you simply want to stand still like a stone, holding up two static pads in a completely unresponsive way and getting your pupil to hit them, monotonously, with an unvarying repertoire. People do it – but how boring is that?

So, take the time when starting out to get things right. This *Complete Guide* will set you on the best path, beginning from the very basics, like stance and guard, right through to more complex punching combinations, footwork, and advanced skipping and focus pad drills. It will be well worth your while to work through the step-by-step instructions and, even if you have some boxing training experience, to check that no technical errors have crept in that are adversely affecting your work.

7

// TEACHING STANCE

Stance is simply the term for the way in which a boxer stands. You will need to learn the correct stance, both to teach your client and for yourself, so that you are in the most effective position when holding the focus pads.

A good stance allows a boxer to punch with power and speed while staying grounded and stable. It also enables him or her to move around nimbly in different directions without losing or compromising their balance. This is known as *footwork* and is covered in more detail in Chapter 8.

BEST FOOT FORWARD

Boxers stand with one foot further forward than the other. It doesn't matter which foot, but they need to choose one! If they opt to put the left foot forward, the term for this stance is orthodox. If they stand with their right foot in front, it is known as a southpaw stance – shown in figure 7.1. In fact, the terminology is irrelevant, but it's an interesting nugget to pass on to your clients. Saying, 'oh, if you stand like that you're a southpaw', or 'that left foot forwards means you're an orthodox boxer' can add to the allure of learning a new skill.

It used to be that right-handed people would automatically be taught to box orthodox – probably because if the left foot is in front, the left hand

Figure 7.1 Full body stance – southpaw.

Figure 7.2 Position of the lower body in the stance – (a) orthodox, (b) southpaw. In amateur boxing, the rear heel is slightly lifted with the bodyweight shifted on to the rear leg (a), as opposed to professionals (b), whose bodyweight is more evenly distributed.

(a)

(b)

is also forward in the *guard* (see below) – which means that the most powerful shot (the *cross/back hand*) comes from the right, and theoretically the strongest, hand. For the same reason, left-handed people would box from the southpaw stance. However, these days such pigeon-holing isn't encouraged: plenty of left-handed people feel more comfortable boxing southpaw and vice versa. The most important thing for you and for your client is to try out both ways and decide on which feels best.

A determining factor in this may be whether your client feels at their most effective when jabbing with the right or the left hand (see pages 43–7). The jab *always* comes from the front hand. So if your student naturally wants to jab with the left, they will put their left hand and left foot in front and box orthodox. If they jab with the right, the opposite applies and they'll box southpaw.

OTHER STANCE CONSIDERATIONS

Figure 7.2 shows the position of the lower body in the stance: (a) is orthodox and (b) southpaw. Here are the key teaching points:

- Once the student has chosen which foot will be in front, instruct them to take a measured step forwards with it. Not a lunge, nor a reach – just a decent step.
- As well as a good distance between the feet lengthways (front to back), there should be space laterally between the feet. If the client steps forwards as if on a tightrope, or 'crosses' their feet when moving around, this will adversely affect their balance and also inhibit the power of their shots.
- The front foot faces slightly inwards, around 45 degrees towards the mid-line of the body. The back foot is correspondingly angled outwards a little (i.e. clockwise for the orthodox stance, and anti-clockwise for the southpaw stance) – to the same approximate 45 degrees as the front foot. Another useful way to think about it is: in the orthodox stance, the feet would be at around ten past the hour on a clock face; in the southpaw stance, both feet would be at around ten to the hour.
- The knees should be loosely bent, but the client shouldn't be crouching, which will strain

Figure 7.3 Full body stance – orthodox.

and tire the muscles: the stance should be a strong, grounded, comfortable position.

- As regards bodyweight distribution, in amateur boxing the heel of the back foot is always held slightly off the floor, with the bodyweight shifted slightly onto the back leg (see figure 7.2a). This aids the boxer's mobility over a relatively small number of competitive rounds. Professional boxers, who may compete over 12 rounds, tend to distribute their bodyweight evenly and shifted onto the balls of the feet, without actually lifting the heel from the floor. It's up to you which method you prefer to teach – but bear in mind that if you are training youngsters who may wish to compete as amateurs, it's advisable to encourage the former stance: that way, they won't have to make later adjustments to their technique.

- At this point it's likely that the client's whole body will be facing forwards. In boxing this is termed being *square on* and it isn't advisable – partly because it exposes the mid-section to perfectly legal *body shots*. The ideal stance is in fact slightly sideways-on to an imaginary opponent, turning the body towards the rear foot while keeping the front foot, hip and shoulders in line. Standing sideways-on also maximises a boxer's reach, or the range of his or her movements, and allows them to twist from the hips when throwing a punch, making it a much more powerful and effective shot. The correct and incorrect positions are both illustrated in figure 8.1, on page 37.

In this position your student has achieved a good lower body stance – but what do they do with their arms?

THE GUARD

An integral part of the stance, the guard is how a boxer holds their arms and hands – the classic 'hands up' position, which literally guards against an opponent's attack. Figure 7.4. shows the position of the upper body in the guard: (a) orthodox and (b) southpaw.

- Direct your client to raise both hands, each making a loose fist (if the fists are clenched, there will be tension in the torso, shoulders and neck). Their elbows should be bent and tucked closely into the body – show them how rotating their fists inwards slightly will naturally bring the elbows down and in.

- If their stance is orthodox, their left hand is held in front of their face, ready to throw the *jab* (see below). Their fist should be at the level of the top of their shoulder, palm facing partially inwards towards the body. If their stance is southpaw, their right hand will be in front in the same position.

- The other (rear/back) hand is held further back, fist close to the chin – protecting it, ready to block a potential punch. The palm faces partially inwards, as with the front hand, with the elbow remaining close to the ribs.

Take the time regularly to review your clients' or pupils' stance, since almost every boxing technique they will learn is performed from it. Errors in the stance can measurably inhibit the effectiveness of their punches and combinations, and even lead indirectly to injury, so it pays to get it right.

CHECKLIST FOR A CORRECT STANCE

Do:

- Make sure their chin is held down, but their eyes always looking up. This is sometimes referred to as 'looking through the eyebrows'.
- Check their shoulders are naturally rolled forwards, with the neck and shoulders relaxed.
- Ensure that they are comfortable and balanced. If they feel or seem otherwise, ask them to stand up straight, 'shake it out', and try again. Get them to 'rock' back and forth until they are used to the feel of a grounded stance.

Don't:

- Let them switch feet (unless it's in the early stages, when they are still trying out both sides to see which feels most natural). If their stance is orthodox, the left foot and hand should always stay in front – and vice versa. There's a good reason for this, from your point of view: when you are holding the pads, for your own safety you need to be sure you know which

(a)   (b)

Figure 7.4 The guard: (a) orthodox and (b) southpaw.

hand they are going to jab with! If they switch stance without warning, you'll hold up the wrong pad for the jab and may end up with a face full of glove.

- Allow them to carry too much weight over their front foot – even going so far as to lean forwards. When they start punching, they may be tempted to add momentum to the shot by lunging forwards; this will leave them unbalanced and unable quickly to return to the stance ready for the next punch or combination.
- Let any tension creep into their arms, shoulders and neck. If you see their shoulders rising, emphasising the need for a 'long neck' can help.

Once you are happy with your client's stance, you need to progress to basic footwork. In boxing, it's no good just standing beautifully – you have to be able to get out of the way!

TEACHING
FOOTWORK

8

Even in a non-contact environment, it's vital to take on board the fact that hitting an opponent is only part of the skill of boxing. At least as important is not getting hit – and this necessitates:

- Deft footwork, to get yourself out of the way of your opponent's attacking shots, and to position yourself ideally for your own offensives.
- A range of defensive manoeuvres to block, ward off or avoid any blows that come your way.

If you are competing, the aim is to prevent your opponent's shots from landing on your head or body. This is because (a) you don't want them to score points and therefore possibly win the bout, and (b) you definitely don't want their attacks to hurt or incapacitate you.

It may not be so obvious, however, that footwork and defence are also important elements in boxing fitness. Static drills and combinations are fine, in and of themselves, but they are limited: you can add a whole new dimension to your clients' workouts by introducing movement between the punches and combinations.

This added dimension is not only cardiovascular. By moving around more, you are of course increasing the muscles' need for oxygen and thus increasing the work done by the heart and lungs, leading to positive cardiorespiratory adaptation. But there are other benefits, such as improved balance, agility, coordination and reaction time. These skills transfer to many other sports, and also aid functional fitness – training your body to handle real-life actions and situations with reduced fatigue and risk of injury.

Remember that you are learning to box, and teaching your clients to box, in order to practise boxing fitness at its most effective. So you *all* need to incorporate movement skills in your shadow boxing, punch bag and focus pad work to get the most out of your joint sessions and programmes.

BASIC FOOTWORK

Boxers try to remain in their stance at all times, even when on the move between punches – i.e. when engaged in footwork – and for good reasons.

As we have already seen on page 34, a common fault, especially in beginners, is to turn *square on* to an opponent; in other words, to position the whole body facing forwards, with the mid-section exposed and thus vulnerable to attacking body shots. When you are square on, no matter how clever you are defensively with your guard, it's not

Figure 8.1 (a) shows the correct technique, with the mid-section turned sideways-on and thus protected from body shots. (b) is incorrect – the stance is too 'square on' to the imaginary opponent.

possible at all times to protect the full target area made by your body.

Ideally, then, the boxer will stand with their mid-section slightly sideways-on to their opponent, turning the lower body towards the rear foot while keeping the front foot, hip and shoulders in line as illustrated in figure 8.1a. As well as afford-ing them protection, this position maximises their reach and allows them to pivot from the hips when throwing punches, delivering much more powerful and effective shots.

Because defence is an integral part of the skill of boxing, the sideways-on stance is maintained even during footwork. This is achieved with a kind of 'push step', which is in effect more like a shift, or a shuffle, than an actual pace in any direction. It is definitely easier to do when moving forwards or backwards: with novices, and even with more experienced boxers, a shift to the square-on position happens most often when they are attempting to travel laterally – since stepping sideways with either their lead or their rear leg will inevitably widen the distance between the feet, squaring up the hips, however momentarily.

MOVING FORWARDS AND BACKWARDS

Here are some tips for teaching your client how to advance and retreat – known in boxing as 'moving in and out' (in, towards your opponent, to throw attacking punches; out, away from the range of a counterattack – in other words, switching between offensive and defensive boxing).

As the student practises their basic footwork, check their stance and their guard. Are the hands close to the chin, with the chin tucked down? Are the eyes looking up and ahead? The elbows should be close to the body, with the shoulders rounded forwards a little and the knees slightly bent. If you are teaching potential amateur boxers, make sure the back heel remains off the floor at all times, with the bodyweight shifted onto the rear leg and the rear knee loosely bent (see also pages 33–4). Under no circumstance should your client bend forwards at the hips.

- To move forwards (advance), instruct them simply to step forwards a little with their lead foot. It's not a lunge; it's a small step or shift of a few inches only, encouraged via a slight push off the ball of the back foot. Too large a step and they will be off balance, as well as risking

a flat-footed 'heel-toe' action with the front foot, inhibiting their mobility.

- The front foot maintains the 45-degree inwards angle of the stance; the toes should not be pointing directly forwards. The back foot mirrors this, with the heel raised slightly to facilitate the shift forwards once the front foot has moved (see next point).
- When they have stepped with the front foot, they simply slide or shift their rear foot forwards to follow it. The aim is to return the body to the exact same position as when they started, but a few inches further forwards. The action is then repeated to continue the advance.
- To move backwards, they simply reverse the above – stepping backwards with the rear foot, via a slight push off the ball of the front foot, and then moving the front foot back to regain the stance. The same technical cautions apply.

Some common errors to look out for – and tips for correcting them

- They fail to maintain a gap laterally between the legs, as emphasised in the section on stance. A common fault is to step too far *across* the body, so the client is in effect 'walking a tightrope' and loses the solid, balanced feel of the stance. They might even allow the legs/feet to cross over.

    Tip: Bring them back to the stance and re-emphasise the importance to their balance of maintaining a consistent space – shoulder-width or slightly wider – between the feet. If you have masking tape, lay two parallel lines along the floor like a train track, spaced appropriately, and ask them to place one foot on each line, then try again (see figure 8.2). Or use the lines on a basketball court.

- They lean forwards at the hips, bringing their bodyweight too far forwards – which will put them off-balance.

Tip: Try teasing them, asking if they're on the lookout for spare change on the floor! Suggest that they extend the front knee a little (not going so far as to 'lock' the joint); this should bring the bodyweight back to the correct place.

Figure 8.2 You can use lines of masking tape to keep an appropriate distance between the feet as the client practises their footwork.

- They do the opposite, standing too upright or even leaning back, with stiff, rigid legs instead of softly bent knees.

Tip: Place your hands on their shoulders and push them backwards (gently!). Inevitably, they will overbalance. Then guide them into the correct body position and repeat – their balance will be demonstrably better.

- They repeatedly bring the feet too far together (front to back, as opposed to sideways), widening and narrowing the distance between the lead and rear foot instead of keeping this as constant as possible. Again, this will impinge on their balance. Or, they leave the 'following' foot way behind, so that it has to be dragged back into the stance.

Tip: Stress that only a few inches is travelled with each step. Go back to basics; recap the key teaching points for the stance, and demonstrate how the correct 'push step' enables this to be maintained, even during multi-directional movement (see below).

MOVING FROM SIDE TO SIDE

When they have practised moving forwards and backwards, progress to lateral footwork. They may find this a little more awkward. The main thing to stress to your client is that whichever direction they intend to travel – to their right or left – the foot closest to that direction steps first.

So, if they are going right, and are in the orthodox stance:

- Instruct them to step to the right with their rear foot initially, again only a few inches – maintaining the slight outward angle of the foot (see figure 8.3b).

- They then bring the left (front) foot quickly to follow it – same direction, same distance – to move the body over and regain their original stance (see figure 8.3c).
- Ask them to note that they'll need to do this a little more swiftly than when moving in and out because, necessarily, when they step to one side their hips open out and they are temporarily more square-on to their imaginary opponent.

- To move back to their left, they will step in that direction with their lead leg, following with the right to bring their body back into the stance.

Southpaws travelling to the right will step with their front (right) foot first; when moving to their left, it is the rear (left) foot that leads.

Similar, common errors may occur as discussed in the section above: for example, they may step

Figure 8.3 Moving to the right in an orthodox stance. The rear (right) foot push-steps a few inches (b), with the lead (left) foot quickly following it to regain the stance.

too far over and have to drag the 'following' foot to rejoin its fellow, over-straighten the legs, bend forwards at the hips, and so on. There is no need to repeat all the technical cautions: you will have got the message. Simply work through the checklist with patience, and encourage them not to get frustrated.

Boxing footwork doesn't feel natural at first. If your client is struggling, acknowledge this and emphasise the need for practice. Incorporating some basic footwork in shadow boxing, punch bag and focus pad work as early as possible can help reinforce the correct technique as well as optimising aerobic fitness gains during sessions.

Remind them, too, that the position and movements involved in boxing footwork is great exercise for the core and lower body, toning and strengthening the abdominals, obliques, gluteals and inner thighs. Eventually this odd kind of rolling or push-stepping action becomes second nature, and they will be able to speed things up, moving in different directions fluidly and with ease.

If and when your student becomes more confident, you can start to introduce the punches, singly and in combination (see pages 42–67); you can also progress on to more complex footwork so that they become fluent when moving in any and all directions. Below is one example of a fun footwork drill; others are covered in Chapter 12 on defence.

- The client moves their rear foot slightly 'behind' them (but only a few inches) – travel clockwise for orthodox, anti-clockwise for southpaw.
- Almost simultaneously they then pivot the ball of their front foot and their lead hip, in the same direction, effectively retrieving the balanced stance.
- Perhaps they throw some punches or combinations before continuing – eventually 'circling' an imaginary opponent.
- Explain that it is as if their front foot were the centre-point of a clock, and their rear foot moving around the outside of the clock's face. A line drawn between their front and rear foot would be the clock's hand.
- You can even get them to try reversing the direction, moving their *front* foot first: it's a challenge!

As well as practising specific footwork drills with your clients, you can further improve their mobility, coordination and balance with skipping (see Chapter 13).

TEACHING THE PUNCHES: STRAIGHT SHOTS

9

There are four main punches to learn and teach: the *jab*; the *cross* (called the back hand in amateur boxing); the *hook*; and the *uppercut*. The first two are known as straight shots: hooks and uppercuts are known as bent-arm shots.

All four punches can be delivered singly or in various *combinations*. A combination is defined as more than a single punch thrown consecutively – in other words, two or more shots strung together, sometimes referred to as 'punches in bunches'! Building complex combinations of increasing duration, varying speed and incorporating footwork is a fantastic way of increasing your clients' cardiorespiratory fitness and muscle endurance, as well as challenging and stimulating them mentally.

Note: Check beforehand that the client or student doesn't mind being touched appropriately in order to correct any minor positional errors. It's highly unlikely that they will, but if you've asked the question then you're covered. This is something you may wish to address during your preliminary consultation (see pages 20–1) to eliminate any potential awkwardness later on in your trainer/client relationship.

A quick reminder that *you need to know how to punch* before teaching anyone else. In a way, you might work through this book twice: once, to teach yourself the basics of boxing; and then again to pick up the key points for teaching someone else. When you have started practising the punches and combinations with your clients, they will be keen to start hitting the focus pads as soon as possible; so at this stage you already need to be confident with your own technique (see also Part Three).

But don't be tempted to run before you can walk: it's important to master the basics first.

For this reason, in this chapter the two straight shots – the jab and the cross/back hand – are broken down into detailed teaching points, accompanied by illustrations, to enable you to communicate the correct technique to your client or student. Always begin with these punches: don't progress to hooks and uppercuts (discussed in Chapter 10) until the straight shots can be solidly and reliably delivered.

When teaching any punch or combination, it's best both to 'show and tell': to use a mixture of clear, spoken teaching points and practical demonstration.

THE JAB

This is the first punch to learn and teach; it is the most important shot in boxing – and in boxing fitness. Boxers use the jab for many different effects: to find their range; to control and unsettle an opponent; to set up and finish combinations; and, singly or in multiples, as a highly effective attacking shot. The jab can be thrown to the head and to the body.

From your point of view, the most important thing to emphasise about the jab is that it is *always delivered from the front hand*. In an orthodox stance, your client will jab with their left; southpaws will jab with their right. If they mix this up when on the focus pads, you risk holding up the wrong mitt and possibly getting hit. Things can also become very confusing, especially bearing in mind that you are working opposite your client – who may additionally be working in a different stance from the one you prefer.

Here are the main teaching points for the jab, followed by some common errors and how to correct them. There are quite a lot of the latter, which reflects just how important it is to get this essential foundation punch perfect and polished.

• Check your client's stance and guard (see pages 32–5). Instruct them to push into the floor

with the ball of the front foot while making a slight, fast turn of the lead hip inwards. The hips naturally rotate towards the rear leg.

- Simultaneously, tell them to throw out their lead (front) hand until the arm is fully extended. The movement comes straight out from the shoulder, and the hand remains at shoulder level. The elbow must stay down, close to

Figure 9.2 The jab: (a) orthodox and (b) southpaw.

the body rather than being lifted laterally away from it.

- The rear hand is kept up in a defensive position, close to the chin, with the chin tucked down and the elbow close to the body.
- As their jab arm extends and accelerates towards the target, they should rotate the wrist so that at the last point before contact, at the end of the movement, their hand is facing palm-down.
- At the point of impact, the *knuckled* part of their hand (i.e. the knuckles and the first joint of the four fingers) makes straight and true contact with the punch bag, focus pad or imaginary opponent. The thumb remains naturally curled in, touching the second joint of the index finger.
- Immediately after their jab has reached its full extension, they reverse the movement *keeping the arm along the same line as the shot was thrown* – i.e. without allowing the hand to drop – thus returning their hand to its original guard position.

As clients progress with their boxing fitness, the jab may be used to develop speed and power, to practise defence, and to make contact with the punch bag and focus pads at different levels and in different positions. In the early stages, however, focus on helping them achieve good technique and build the jab into a strong, confident shot.

Some common errors to look out for – and tips for correcting them

- The wrist joint is not kept 'strong', but rather bends – either hand-downwards, so the back of the hand makes the contact; or hand-upwards, so the client ends up 'slapping' with the inside of the wrist or finger ends.

Tip: Re-emphasise the straight line made by the arm all the way from shoulder to first knuckle joints, and demonstrate once again the correct contact point of the fist against the pad or your own palm (see figure 9.3).

- After the contact, as they bring the hand back to the guard they allow it to drop, resulting in a kind of downwards circling movement of the hand. In boxing, this would simply invite a swift counterpunch to the chin!

  Tip: Stress that the hand returns to the guard along the same line as it travelled out. Straight out, straight back. If they are working on the focus pads, you could gently tap the pad out to touch their exposed chin as the hand drops… thus making your point quite clear.

- They fail to rotate the wrist palm-downwards just before the point of contact. This shortens the punch because it doesn't engage the shoulder/deltoid; weakens it because it doesn't engage the triceps; and risks injury to the arm because the elbow joint doesn't lock.

  Tip: As above. Demonstrate how engaging and extending the shoulder turns the wrist naturally in the correct direction; and remind them about the martial arts 'one inch punch' – the generation of incredible power through short muscle action at close range.

- The elbow is lifted laterally, away from the body towards the horizontal. This changes the angle of the hand so that the outside – and especially the little-finger knuckle joint – makes the contact. The effect is to telegraph and weaken the shot (it becomes a kind of mix of jab and hook), and

potentially to cause soreness and even injury to the hand or wrist.

Tip: Remind them that the jab extends from the shoulder and the elbow stays close to the body for as long as possible during the movement. Emphasising the wrist rotation just before the point of contact can help, as can re-demonstrating the optimal position of the knuckled part of the fist against your pad or own palm.

- The jab is weak and static, with no 'snap' or power behind it. It becomes an 'arm punch'.

  Tip: Emphasise the importance of extending the shoulder joint forwards to achieve more range in the movement. Stress the importance of the initial turn of the front hip inwards with a slight push off the front foot.

Figure 9.3 The knuckled part of the fist makes contact – the hand facing palm-down and the thumb loosely curled in.

- They 'lunge' off the back foot to get some momentum behind the punch, leaning forwards and over-committing to the shot with too much of their bodyweight. In the boxing ring, this will leave them unbalanced and vulnerable, attempting to return to the stance as their opponent sends a swift and effective counterpunch their way.

Tip: Re-ground their stance, bringing the bodyweight back with no bend at the hips but loose bend at the knees. Emphasise that it is the correct punching technique, combined with the front-foot push and lead-hip movement, which generates the power.

THE JAB TO THE BODY

This shot uses exactly the same technique as described above, but before it is delivered, the knees are bent so that the jab lands to the imaginary opponent's body instead of their head.

As shown in Figure 9.4, the client should 'sit' into the movement, rather than bending the back or over at the hips. If they find this difficult, suggest they imagine sitting straight down into a chair – or, if they are familiar with weight/resistance training, it is just like a shallow squat. Point out that the movement is great for toning all the large muscle groups of the lower body – and, for exactly this reason, burns calories!

Figure 9.4 Jab to the body: (a) southpaw and (b) orthodox.

For the jab to the body, the order of movement is this:

- Stance
- 'Sit'
- Jab
- Return jab hand to the guard
- Rise back into the stance

Break the shot down into its component parts, before starting to put it together, so that it becomes a fluid and rapid technique. It's useful to get this squatting motion mastered, because it is also used in defence (see Chapter 12), and you can employ it in any number of boxing fitness drills to increase their efficacy.

THE CROSS (BACK/REAR HAND)

So-termed because it is delivered from the back hand, across the body. Working from an orthodox stance, the cross will be thrown with the rear (right) hand, so is sometimes known as the straight right. In amateur boxing the cross is referred to as the back hand.

Because the cross/back hand has the weight of the body turning into the shot, as the hips and torso twist, it is a very powerful punch and accounts for a large percentage of knockdowns and knockouts in boxing. It can be really therapeutic for your clients and pupils to realise they can hit as hard as they like with this shot, as soon as they've mastered the technique. Working on the focus pads with kids, you can motivate them with something like: 'C'mon – seriously? Is that all you've got?' Watch them let fly… much better on your pad, or the heavy bag, than on anything (worse, anyone) else.

Figure 9.5 The cross/back hand – orthodox stance.

- Check your client's stance and guard (see pages 32 and 35 respectively). Instruct them to push off the ball of the rear foot, simultaneously rotating the hips strongly in the direction of the punch. The torso naturally follows suit, so that the whole body is in effect rotating around a central, vertical axis – anti-clockwise for orthodox, clockwise for southpaw. The front knee bends slightly to enable this.
- At the same time as they initiate the rear leg drive, with the front hand held close to the chin, instruct them to throw the rear hand forwards towards an imaginary opponent's head. Because they are standing sideways-on, as already discussed, it comes naturally to deliver the shot across the body.

- As with the jab, during the punching movement they will rotate their arm so when it is fully extended – at the moment of 'impact' – the knuckles are uppermost and the palm facing down. It is the knuckled part of the glove which makes contact, with a closed fist.
- When the arm has reached its full extension, it is then retracted by reversing the movement and bringing the hand back to the guard position. Make sure this is done along the same line as the shot was thrown – in other words, don't let your student drop their hand after the punch.
- Point out to them that the hip movement is an integral part of the cross/back hand. If they simply punch out using their arm alone, they can achieve very little power or reach – it's more like a karate-type shot. Twisting the hips and shoulders into the punch generates power through the body, and out through the closed fist.

Some common errors to look out for – and tips for correcting them

- As with the jab, the wrist joint is not kept straight and strong.
  Tip: Re-emphasise the straight line made by the arm all the way from shoulder to first knuckle joints, and demonstrate once again the correct contact point of the fist against the pad or your own palm.

- As with the jab, the elbow is lifted laterally, away from the body, straying into the territory of the hook.
  Tip: Remind them that the cross/back hand extends from the shoulder and the elbow stays close to the body for as long as possible during the movement; also that it is

the strong, knuckled part of the fist which makes contact.

- The shot is weak and static, with no power behind it.
  Tip: Emphasise the importance of pivoting the hips and shoulders into the movement, extending the shoulder joint forwards to achieve more range. Also, draw their attention to the rear foot, which should turn slightly to encourage the hip movement.

- The back foot leaves the ground entirely, adversely affecting balance and shifting the bodyweight too far forwards.
  Tip: Remind them they're not doing ballet! Suggest they consider a kind of bolt, fixed through the front part of the rear foot and screwing into the floor. They can – should –

Figure 9.6 The cross/back hand – southpaw stance, showing the importance of extending the shoulder for power and range.

raise the heel a little and pivot the foot around the bolt in order to initiate the hip rotation, but the foot can't be lifted up.

- They neglect to bring the active hand back snappily into the guard, instead leaving the arm extended for too long.
  Tip: Tell them not to stand and admire their shot! If they did that in the ring, their opponent would take full advantage with a nasty counter. In boxing fitness, they need to return speedily to the guard in order to follow with the next punch or combination, to achieve a good flow in their work.

THE CROSS/BACK HAND TO THE BODY

As with the jab, the cross to the body requires a 'sit' into the movement, generated by bending the knees:

- Stance
- 'Sit'
- Cross/back hand
- Return rear hand to the guard
- Rise back into the stance

STRAIGHT-SHOT COMBINATIONS: AN INTRODUCTION

Combinations (the term refers to two or more consecutive punches: for example, the basic one-two, or jab followed by a cross/back hand, is a combination) are covered in detail in Chapter 11. But it's wise, before teaching the hook and uppercut as discussed in the next section, to introduce some simple straight-shot combinations to your client.

By practising these, they will begin to see how punches fit together with the whole body working in a balanced way to create momentum, flow, speed and power. Build in some basic footwork and defence (see Chapters 8 and 12), and you have the foundation of their first effective round of shadow boxing, punch bag and focus pad work.

When working with youngsters in particular, you may spend many weeks or months focusing on the straight shots in their various combinations. In amateur boxing, the entire first level of the governing body's coaching course is limited to the jab and back hand and their defences (see Chapter 12) – since a boxer's success depends to a large degree on these two shots, delivered accurately as scoring punches to the head and body, in conjunction with excellent footwork and defence. If youngsters get a good grounding in these skills from the outset, they will be safer as well as more likely to reach their full potential in the sport.

On pages 60–1 there is a table of ten basic combinations, with a name, description and some key teaching points for each. The first five combinations in this table are straight-shot combinations:

- double jab
- one-two
- double jab-cross/back hand
- three straight (jab-cross/back hand-jab)
- four straight (jab-cross/back hand-jab-cross/back hand)

As soon as your pupils or clients have mastered the jab and cross/back hand correctly, let them loose on some or all of these; it's gratifying to see their enthusiasm as they start to feel they are really boxing.

TEACHING THE PUNCHES: HOOKS AND UPPERCUTS

10

Once your client is well versed in the straight shots – the jab and the cross/back hand, to the head and to the body, singly and in combination – you may decide to progress to teaching the bent-arm punches: i.e. hooks and uppercuts. These techniques can be difficult to learn and teach correctly, but will significantly increase the variety and challenge of your boxing fitness repertoire.

Alternatively, you may choose to address the defences first, as covered in Chapter 12. There is an argument for doing so, especially if your pupil or client may wish to box competitively as an amateur at some point in the future. Amateur boxing places the safety of participants as its top priority, and no young person should be allowed in the ring without the ability to defend him- or herself.

For the purposes of boxing fitness alone, the order in which you teach the skills is up to you. Your client may already know the basics of the hooks and uppercuts, and be keen to include them in their sessions; or you may feel that they need the variety and challenge of a full range of shots to keep them motivated. For ease of use of this *Complete Guide*, the bent-arm techniques will be addressed here, keeping all the punches together.

THE HOOK

The hook can be delivered from the lead or the rear hand. It is sometimes described as a semi-circular punch, designed to make impact with the side of an opponent's head or chin, or with their torso.

LEAD HAND HOOK TO THE HEAD

- Check your client's stance and guard (see pages 32 and 35 respectively).
- This shot is initiated with a fast rotation 'inwards' – towards the body, as it were – of the front hip; the upper body naturally follows suit. As the hips pivot, so does the toe of the front foot: the heel is raised from the floor.
- On initiating the shot, instruct your client simultaneously to lift the elbow of their lead (front) arm laterally, towards the horizontal – so that the elbow and fist are at the same level as their shoulder. The arm remains bent, with a fixed angle of around 90 degrees at the elbow joint.
- The shoulder, arm, wrist and hand all make a straight line, parallel to the floor. The palm of the striking hand is face-down, knuckles uppermost, and the thumb tucked loosely against the index finger. The rear hand is held close into the jaw, to protect the chin.

Figure 10.1 The lead hand hook – southpaw stance.

- The pivot of the hips and upper body in the direction of the shot naturally propels the fist through a tight arc across the front of your client's body, into the point of contact.
- Upon contact, the hook's semi-circular path ends abruptly: the hand is quickly returned to the guard position and the rest of the body rotates back into the stance. Throughout, the back hand is held close into the chin in the guard position, elbow close to the body, chin tucked down and eyes looking ahead.

Note that the angle at the elbow of the active arm may need to vary, depending on your client's distance or range from the target: in boxing, hooks are thrown at close, mid- and long range. Teach the hook as described above, but as your client becomes more proficient you can experiment with the hook at different ranges.

The important thing is that there is always a bend at the elbow which remains fixed during the shot. If the arm is allowed to straighten it becomes a 'slap' which has no power and can risk injury.

REAR HAND HOOK TO THE HEAD

The rear hand hook to the head is performed in the same manner, but obviously with the back hand, pivoting the rear hip and toe of the rear foot. The front hand is held close into the chin in the guard position, elbow close to the body, chin tucked down and eyes looking ahead.

HOOKS TO THE BODY

Both the lead and the rear hand hook can be directed at the body, as well as delivered to the head. For hooks lower down on the torso, the position of the hand may vary from the palm-down, knuckles-uppermost position described above – instead it lands on the target palm-inwards and thumb on top, with the forearm and fist rotated away from the body as shown in Figure 10.2. The resultant hook is a little like the movement you would use to slam a door shut. Make sure it is still the knuckled part of the glove that makes the contact, and that the wrist remains strong so the hand doesn't bend back: this will result in a 'slap' with the inside wrist. Check too that the client maintains a fixed angle at the elbow throughout; if they allow the arm to straighten, they could well jar the elbow or wrist.

Some common errors to look out for – and tips for correcting them

- The client allows the angle between the forearm and upper arm to open excessively. This makes the shot long and looping, easily anticipated, and much less powerful. It also risks an awkward connection with the punch bag or focus pad, with resultant soreness or injury to the hand or wrist.

  Tip: Encourage them to hold a tight right-angle at the elbow joint and demonstrate how the movement is achieved not by an active 'punching out' of the arm and hand, but rather via the power generated by the hip and shoulder twist – through the body, and out through the closed fist.

- The elbow drops below the horizontal, or is raised too high – above the horizontal. With the former, the inside of the hand or wrist makes the contact in a slapping movement. If the latter, they end up punching down, even

Figure 10.2 Lead hand hook to the body – southpaw stance.

Figure 10.3 Correcting the elbow position in the lead hand hook – orthodox stance.

with the back of the hand. Neither is effective, and both risk soreness or worse.

Tip: Demonstrate once again the shoulder, arm, wrist and hand working as a unit, held horizontal and parallel to the ground. It can help to remind them of the correct position of the fist at the point of contact, with the wrist kept strong and the flat, knuckled part of the closed hand striking the bag or glove.

- They drop the hand of the hooking arm, circling it downwards before raising the elbow – telegraphing the shot and leaving their chin exposed. And/or they draw the active shoulder backwards before lifting the elbow, ostensibly to generate momentum for more power.

Tip: Emphasise that it is the elbow which lifts first, straight from the guard. Stress that power is generated by the body rotation – *not* via the punch.

- They don't look where they are punching! If they stare anxiously forwards, without turning the head, how can the hook be performed correctly – given that it requires a fast pivot of the hips, torso and shoulders?

Tip: Encourage them to look at the target, keeping the body and head twisting as a unit but without any tension in the neck and shoulders. As soon as contact has been made with the fist, they should return their focus – along with all other parts of the body – to the front in the correct stance.

- They over-pivot, or over-rotate the body with the shot, which will leave them off-balance, and may even make them spin round,

prohibiting them from returning promptly to the stance.

Tip: Emphasise that *as soon as contact has been made* with the bag, pad or imaginary opponent, it is time to snap the hooking hand back into the guard and return to the stance.

ALTERNATE HAND POSITION

The technique described above is the traditional way to hook – but some people find it extremely hard to achieve, struggling especially with the horizontal position of the forearm and keeping the knuckles of the hand uppermost. In teaching boxing fitness, this difficulty can be the most common cause of awkward contact with the focus pad, and resultant soreness or injury to the thumb or wrist.

While you want to teach correctly and successfully, helping your students to master the basic shots, you *don't* want to frustrate them by constantly picking up on their faults. When this happens they may lose confidence, becoming

Figure 10.4 Alternate hand position for the hook.

anxious about doing it wrong and possibly getting hurt. They can also become a bit resentful because, after all, they really want to box and all this technique stuff is getting in the way.

If this occurs repeatedly with the hook, you have the option of suggesting an alternative method – as mentioned above, under 'Hooks to the body'. In this, the forearm and fist are rotated away from the body, palm-inwards as shown in figure 10.4. The resultant hook is a little like the movement you would use to slam a door shut, and may be easier and more comfortable for your client. Always make sure they keep the fixed angle at the elbow, and that contact is still made with the knuckles, keeping the wrist strong – not with a 'slap' from the inside of the glove.

THE UPPERCUT

The uppercut is the fourth and final punch you will teach your clients. It is the only 'vertical' shot

Figure 10.4 Lead hand uppercut – southpaw stance.

in boxing; rather than being delivered straight out from the guard like the jab and the cross, or around the side like the hook, it is thrown up towards the target – which is generally an opponent's chin, but can also be lower down, on their body.

Like the hook, the uppercut can be thrown with both the lead and the rear hands.

LEAD HAND UPPERCUT

- Check your client's stance and guard (see pages 32 and 35 respectively).
- The power for the shot is generated through the lead leg. The first movement is a sharp push into the floor with the front foot; the knee, which is loosely bent in the stance, extends, as does the lead hip which also pivots – clockwise for orthodox; anti-clockwise for southpaw; the rear hip will follow suit. The front toe may turn slightly in the same direction, and the heel will naturally lift from the floor.
- As they push upwards with the front leg, instruct your client to turn the lead forearm and wrist so that the palm faces inwards, towards their body. This is important, since the knuckled part of the hand – rather than the side, thumb-uppermost – must finish the shot.
- The arm should be kept bent, with a fixed angle at the elbow and the elbow pointing directly at the floor. Remember: the lead hand uppercut is a short, sharp movement with most of the power coming from the front leg, through the hips and out through the fist, rather than being generated by a 'punching' action.
- Remind your client to keep their eye on the target, but with their chin tucked in and protected by the lead shoulder. The rear hand remains close to the chin in the guard, elbow close to the body.

- At the end of the punch, as soon as contact has been made, the lead hand is brought quickly back to the guard position, with all other parts of the body rotating back into the stance.

The teaching points for the rear hand uppercut are also given here, as it has quite a different kind of 'feel' for the client, even though it is performed with the same basic technique. In boxing, the rear hand uppercut is generally only performed at close range to an opponent, 'on the inside', whereas the lead hand shot can be delivered from further out.

REAR HAND UPPERCUT

- Check your client's stance and guard (see pages 32 and 35 respectively).
- As with the lead hand uppercut, the shot is initiated via a strong push upwards with the foot – but this time, with the rear foot. This produces a strong drive up through the leg, which extends the back knee and causes rotation of the hips: anti-clockwise for orthodox; clockwise for southpaw. The rear toe may pivot in the same direction, and the heel is naturally raised from the floor.
- At the same as they are driving up with their back leg, instruct the client to rotate the forearm and wrist of their back hand so that the palm faces inwards, towards their body. Again, this is important, since the knuckled part of the hand – rather than the side, thumb-uppermost – must finish the shot.
- The upward arc made by the fist will necessarily be wider than for the lead hand uppercut, in order to make contact from further back; however, the arm should still be kept bent, with a fixed angle at the elbow. Remember: most of the power for the rear uppercut comes

Figure 10.5 Rear hand uppercut – southpaw stance.

from the back leg, through the hips and out through the fist, rather than being generated by the 'punch' itself. The bodyweight is firmly over the rear leg.
- Remind your client to keep their eye on the target, and their chin tucked in and protected by the rear shoulder. The front hand remains close to the chin in the guard, elbow held close to the body.

- At the end of the punch, the rear hand is brought quickly back to the guard position, with all other parts of the body rotating back into the stance.

Some common errors to look out for – and tips for correcting them

- The client throws the uppercut with a straightened arm, resulting in a loopy, weak and easily anticipated shot, and/or a slapping contact with the palm of the hand or wrist, rather than the knuckled fist. They may even 'wind up' their shot if they've seen this done on TV by showboating professional boxers!

  Tip: Emphasise the fixed angle at the elbow, and the fact that power is generated not via an active punching movement (i.e. arm extension), but by the legs, through the hips, and out through the fists.

- They drop the hand too low before beginning the upward thrust of the shot. This would leave them open to an opponent's counterpunch before their fist had even met its intended target.

  Tip: As above. Suggest they think about keeping the 'active' hand close to the chin, and the elbow of the same side close to the body, for a beat after the leg drive and hip rotation have begun; only then does the elbow thrust out from the 'active' hip.

- They omit the leg drive and focus on the arm movement, so there is no power or drive behind the shot.

  Tip: Try suggesting they imagine a strong pushing force emanating from beneath the floor, rising upwards through their driving foot, up the leg and into the hips. Stress the importance of the bodyweight shift on to the ball of the front foot for the lead hand uppercut, and on the back leg for the rear hand uppercut. Actually *show* them how difficult it is to achieve the shot successfully with rigid legs, relying on the arm with its fixed angle at the elbow joint. Don't, however, let them over-compensate with a deep squat, which can strain the leg muscles and will actually slow the uppercut down, telegraphing the shot.

- They fail to turn the hand sufficiently palm-inwards, so that contact is made with the side of the hand and the thumb. This can really injure the thumb, so it's important to nip this fault in the bud at an early stage.

  Tip: You can try suggesting a very slight drop or 'dip' of the shoulder of the punching arm: try it yourself and you'll see that this naturally begins a turn of the hand in towards the body. Don't let them over-emphasise this, however, or it risks turning into a lateral bend of the body at the waist adversely affecting balance and bodyweight distribution.

Obviously, it's usually only advisable to demonstrate correct technique to your client or student, so as not to inadvertently fix any fault in their mind: the value of positive role modelling and visualisation is well documented. But sometimes it can help to actually show them what they're doing wrong, using a little exaggeration to highlight the fault's negative impact on their boxing. Then, follow this with a clear, slow, repeated demonstration of the right technique in order to show the difference.

TEACHING THE COMBINATIONS

11

The four main punches described in Chapters 9 and 10 can be thrown in isolation (e.g. a single jab; a straight cross/back hand); repeated (e.g. double jab; double hook); or mixed up in groups known as combinations (e.g. double jab followed by a cross/back hand).

Although it's tempting to do so, avoid progressing on to complex combinations with your client until you're reasonably happy with their technique for the individual shots. Even when they're familiar with each punch, things can go awry as they start stringing them together because there's so much to think about. This is part of the learning process – for them and for you – and gets much easier with time and practice.

Learning combinations is fun, and challenges you and your students both mentally and physically. In the ring, the most eye-catching combinations are performed fluidly, at high speed and with technical expertise. Boxers can make it look simple, but in fact it's extremely tiring: competitors who fail to pace themselves through a round (and three minutes is a long, long time in a boxing ring), throwing too many fast combinations and power punches, will soon become exhausted, unable to keep their hands up in defence and to move out of the way of their opponent's counterattacks.

The fact that boxing is so physically and psychologically challenging is good news for the exercise professional, since it gives you an almost endless array of options for tiring your client or pupil while keeping them mentally engaged. As they get fitter, you simply (a) allow them less rest and/or (b) make them work harder, faster and/or for longer, to raise their heart rate and fatigue their muscles. Positive training adaptations are therefore always easily within reach: there's no reason for anyone to reach a plateau or get bored.

But if you start too quickly, with too complicated a combination, students can lose confidence or motivation. There is always a balance to achieve: take things too slowly, and risk impatience; progress too fast, and risk frustration as well as potential injury, as technical faults creep in. It's down to *you* to ask the right questions, to listen and to observe your clients' reactions as they learn, and always to offer encouragement and positive feedback.

START WITH THE BASICS – AND PRACTISE

In boxing fitness, combinations can be taught and practised with or without footwork, and in one of three ways:

- As part of a shadow boxing routine
- On the focus pads
- On the punch bag

Each of these boxing fitness elements are covered in this book. Bear in mind that the standard punch bag is only ideal for teaching and practising straight shots and combinations; there are specialised bags for working the uppercuts and hooks. Even using these bags, it can be hard to achieve the correct angle: for bent-arm punches the focus pads are probably the best option.

Whichever method you choose for introducing the combinations, make sure the client starts in the correct stance and completes each punch in the sequence properly, so that it sets them up for the next. Boxing combinations should *flow*; they feel right when delivered well. For this reason alone, they can't be over-practised.

Get your clients to repeat each combination until it becomes second nature. When they've done some footwork and know how to move in the boxing stance (see Chapter 8), practise the same combinations – you might also refer to them as *drills* – going forwards, backwards and to both sides. If they moan about the repetition and are impatient to move on to bigger and better things, explain that it really does pay to do the drills until muscle memory is established. Mastering the basics now will free them up all the more quickly to enjoy increasingly complicated and challenging routines. Ask which is their favourite drill – the one they really get into – and let them start and finish the session with that. Find a way that works, without letting them off the hard stuff.

NAMES OR NUMBERS?

Some boxing trainers, guides and DVDs give every punch a number (the jab = 1, the cross/back hand = 2, the lead hand hook = 3, etc.). They then express each combination fully in numerical form: for example, double jab-cross/back hand will be written or spoken as 1-1-2.

In this book, combinations are referred to mainly by the *name* of the component shots. The exception to this rule is the straight punches – the jab and the cross/back hand – which, when performed in combination, are referred to thus: *one-two* (jab-cross/back hand); *three straight* (jab-cross/back hand-jab); and *four straight* (jab-cross/back hand-jab-cross/back hand). Naming the punches may seem a bit clumsy, but it does help the novice learn the proper terminology. The wholly numerical system can also be confusing, especially for people just starting out.

Of course it's up to you to develop your preferred system for calling out combinations during training. Whatever you choose, make it clear and consistent: asking for *1-2-3-2* one minute and then calling out *jab-cross/back hand-hook-cross/back hand* the next is a sure-fire route to chaos. When you and your client are used to training with each other, and get really good on the focus pads, you may develop a way of communicating non-verbally with small visual signs or signals indicating the punches and combinations to follow. Watch competitive boxers warming up 'backstage' with their trainers and you'll see this kind of synchronised teamwork – it's great to witness.

'TOO LATE, MATE!'

You can also work on clients' reaction times by holding up the focus pads suddenly, with or without any verbal direction, and getting them to respond with the appropriate punch or simple straight-shot combination as quickly as possible. If they respond too slowly, the pad is back down already – 'Too late, mate!'

Make sure you hold up the correct pad for the shot you want. If the client is orthodox, you will raise the left pad for the jab; the right pad for the cross/back hand; and both pads together for the automatic one-two. If they are southpaw, you'll hold up the right pad for the jab and the left for the cross/back hand.

Try moving around yourself while doing this, using your own good footwork, so the client has to get themselves into the right position relative to the pad as well as thinking about which shot to deliver. This is fantastic exercise for all clients and especially for youngsters, who find it a real challenge. Glove-and-pad work is covered in detail in Part Three of this book, with technical considerations for the trainer as well as lots of ideas for varied, interesting drills to work on people's individual development areas.

In terms of the combinations, however, until you yourself are sure what you're asking for, *keep things simple*. You can still give your student a great workout by putting together the most basic combinations in inventive ways (some suggestions are given below); there's no need to put yourself under unnecessary pressure to impress.

This is especially true of focus pad work. Are you definitely ready to string together complex combinations, bearing in mind that this involves (a) thinking them up, (b) calling them out, (c) getting the pads in the right place quickly enough and (d) watching the client to give good feedback about their technique? All the while standing southpaw for a southpaw client when you yourself prefer to box orthodox? It's not easy.

Take your time to learn the trade, and give yourself a break.

ONE COMBINATION AT A TIME – STATIC DRILLS

Even though your client will be eager to learn, don't rush to introduce a whole range of new combinations at once. Start with one, and get that right before progressing to the next. This is important because once they become proficient you will start stringing combinations together; if they are weak in one, it will affect their focus and technique, and thereby inhibit the flow of all the others.

For each new combination you teach your client, practise it first as a *static drill* – i.e. with no footwork (see also Part Three). Remind them of the key technical points for each individual punch and then describe how to put them together. Demonstrate the actions in slow motion, standing next to the student rather than opposite so they can emulate you. Even if you work out of the same stance, with you facing them it may be harder for them to pick up which part of your

Note: in Table 11.1, for the straight shots, the rear/back hand punch is described simply as a *cross* for ease and brevity of reference. Bear in mind that if you are training a current or potential amateur boxer, you will term the straight rear hand punch a *back hand*.

Table 11.1	Basic punching combinations	
Name	**Description**	**Comments**
Straight-shot combinations (see pages 42–9)		
Double jab	Two jabs in quick succession	At first the client may tend to rush or 'paw' at the punches. Get them to take their time, extending the lead arm to its full reach before bringing the fist back to the guard and then delivering the second jab. Using the correct technique for each jab, as described in Chapter 9, will ensure that the double jab shots are sharp and snappy. You can also introduce the *triple jab* – three jabs in quick succession, which is more challenging.
One-two	A jab, followed by a cross	In this combination they may make the mistake of trying to put loads of power into both shots, giving them equal weight. In fact, the drive behind the *one-two* is delivered with the rear hand; the jab is a lighter shot which 'sets up' the combination. When the lead arm has reached its full extension in the jab, and the hand is coming back to the chin, they should begin to throw the cross from the rear hand. The second punch should follow on smoothly from the first (i.e. *one-two* not *one. two.*): the momentum carries the back hand through. Remember to stress the importance of hip rotation in generating power in the cross.
Double jab-cross	Two jabs in succession, followed by a cross	Just as it sounds: the double jab as described above, followed by a powerful, driving cross from the rear hand.
Three straight	A jab followed by a cross, finishing with another jab	Your client performs the *one-two* as described above, adding a final jab. They should aim for a smooth transition from punch to punch; their shoulders, torso and hips need to pivot fluidly with a nicely balanced bodyweight throughout the combination.
Four straight	Jab-cross-jab-cross	As for the *three straight*, but finishing with a final cross – fluid and balanced.

Table 11.1	Basic punching combinations (*cont.*)	
Name	**Description**	**Comments**
Introducing the hooks (see pages 50–4)		
One-two-hook	A jab, followed by a cross, and then a hook with the lead hand	The client performs the *one-two* as described above – a jab followed by a cross – and then adds a lead hand hook (left hook for orthodox, right for southpaw). Remind them of the key points for throwing the hook: elbow up, fixed angle at the elbow joint, and a powerful pivot of the hips into the shot. Eye on the target! Because of the risk of their hand making awkward contact with the focus pad in the early days of learning this combination, get them to perform it slowly first – only picking up speed and power when they are confident about the technique.
Cross-hook-cross	Starting with the back hand, a cross, followed by a lead hand hook, finishing with another cross	This combination omits the initial jab, so your client starts with a strong back hand, following up with a lead hand hook and finishing with another cross. You may need to remind them not to throw the jab! You've spent a long time telling them that they should always lead with the front hand, and this advice will be ingrained: you don't want them to forget, throw a jab, and give you a face full of glove. Emphasise the correct shifts in bodyweight and the hip rotation.
Jab-hook-cross	A jab, followed by a lead (same) hand hook, finished off with a cross	The transition from the jab to the lead hand hook should be smooth but swift, setting the scene nicely for the killer cross that follows!
Introducing the uppercuts (see pages 54–6)		
Jab-uppercut-hook	A jab, followed by a rear hand uppercut, and then a lead hand hook	Pay particular attention to the shifts in bodyweight with these two combinations – each punch leading swiftly to the next via smooth transitions through a balanced stance. For this reason, when repeated, both drills are excellent core training for your client (see also pages 143–50).
Jab-uppercut-hook-cross	As above, but with a strong cross to finish off the combination	

body is doing what. Inevitably some students will be more coordinated than others: don't assume that what comes easily for one will be the same for another. Treat each individual as just that, an individual. With the right amount of support, encouragement and guidance they will all get there in the end.

After demonstrating several times mentally, ask them to try the combination, slowly, as you watch. For their initial attempts, don't introduce a physical target such as the punch bag or focus pad: just get them to go through the correct movements, checking their technique for each component shot against the teaching points given in the relevant chapter(s).

While they are learning, try to judge which errors to pick up on and which it will do no harm to 'let go' for the moment. They won't get everything right first time, and the last thing you want is to dismay them by repeatedly picking holes in each tiny fault. Focus on anything that may be unsafe and lead to injury; you can always fine-tune minor imperfections later. Remember once again: this is boxing *fitness*, and while you all want to get it right, the emphasis is on safety, enjoyment and positive fitness adaptations, not on sporting excellence.

It can be useful to get a client to shadow box their basic combinations in front of a mirror. At the risk of being obvious, this isn't the same as you standing opposite them to demonstrate – because they are actually initiating the movements rather than copying someone else. Boxing in front of a mirror really does highlight faults as well as helping the client judge the accuracy of their shots: they use their own head and body as imaginary targets, as if they were fighting their own outline or shadow – hence the name, shadow boxing (see also Chapter 13).

INTRODUCE A PHYSICAL TARGET

As well as shadow boxing, your students will be keen to actually hit something. Punching even a stationary target is immensely therapeutic; doing it accurately with style and power is even better; and doing all that when your target is moving, so you have to use skilled foot- and bodywork to position yourself for optimal delivery of shots and combinations, is best of all. It is hard, challenging, exhilarating exercise.

In boxing fitness, the physical target can be either the punch bag or the focus pad. (In a group or class setting you can also pair up your students – each wearing sparring gloves – and teach a range of partnered offensive and defensive drills whereby they make very light contact with each other's gloves. This is *not* punching, though – it is technical work which must be done in a carefully supervised environment.)

THE PUNCH BAG

For the straight shots, a punch bag – if you have access to one – is fine. Make sure the bag is sturdy and correctly tethered (see page 17). It shouldn't be so light that it rebounds into your client's face upon the smallest contact. Some punch bags, particularly the free-standing kind, are actually designed to produce rebound, which encourages the boxer to react as if to a counterpunch, using good head movement, defensive skills and footwork to avoid it. But in the early stages of learning to hit something, such bounce-back will be too much, even scary, for your client. If the bag does move around too much, you can always hold on to it, keeping out of your client's way as they work.

In their stance, the client should position themselves at the correct range from the bag – about an arm's length away. If they stand too close, they won't be able to deliver their jab or cross/back hand with full extension. Too far away, and they will be tempted to lunge or lean forwards into their shots, adversely affecting both their technique and balance.

When you're happy with their range, direct them to begin by calling out the shots you want, starting with the basic jab. Don't just tell them to 'hit the bag'; be active and engaged. For example, call out 'Jab! Jab! Double jab! Good – and again! Shake it out now, that's great, hands up, back on the jab! Double it!' They may be stiff and nervous at first. Correct any errors patiently, with a mixture of showing and telling as appropriate, and give loads of encouragement. You can even work

alongside them on the bag, throwing out a jab for them to follow with theirs – whatever keeps them motivated and positive.

Then start to mix in some rear hand shots. 'Throw a big straight right! BOOM! That's good. Try throwing the jab out first, I'm looking for a one-two now. Nice and fluent. Again, but pivot the hip into that rear hand shot – see how the power improves?' And so on. Work them in short bursts to start with, giving them plenty of time to shake out their arms, breathe, resume their stance and guard, and re-focus.

Weirdly enough, lots of novices seem to forget to breathe when they're on the punch bag: you may well find you need to remind them. Deep, controlled, diaphragmatic breathing is important

in boxing, as the large muscle groups work hard and the heart and lungs attempt to keep up with oxygen demand. Your clients *should* be out of breath when they're boxing; just as with any other positive adaptation to exercise, this will significantly improve their cardiorespiratory fitness.

As they start to get the hang of the punch bag, make it more challenging. Get them to punch harder, faster, and/or with less rest. Introduce some footwork (see pages 36–41). Begin to time their efforts, building up until they are able to practise straight shots singly and in combination over two or even three minutes, always with a minute's rest in between.

Remember that even with their hands correctly wrapped inside good-quality gloves, they may experience some chafing of their knuckles and aching or tingling in their hands or wrists the first few times they work the bag. This is normal. But keep an eye out for signs of discomfort and judge carefully when it's time to stop. Some students will be over-careful and others will try to continue even when their hands are sore; it's your job to judge whether to encourage them to keep going or to tell them to stop. If they train until the skin over their knuckles is broken, they will have to take a break from bag and pad work until it heals – and even then, the skin may be more vulnerable to damage for quite a long time afterwards. So err on the side of caution, while reassuring clients that some mild aching is to be expected in those who aren't used to this type of training.

Finally, bear in mind that while boxers do practise hooks and uppercuts on punch bags, this is not ideal for your clients: they're likely to struggle to achieve the correct technique, given the vertical nature of the target and its rounded contours. Keep to the jab and the back hand and their

various combinations – and don't forget that you can also 'work to the body' with both these shots by 'sitting' into them and making contact lower down on the bag. More guidance on punch bag work is given in Chapter 13.

THE FOCUS PADS

When it comes to providing an actual target for your clients to hit as they practise their shots and combinations, it may well be that you don't have access to a suitable punch bag at your training venue. If that's the case – and even if it isn't – oh, the beauty of the focus pads: they travel with you, light and compact, wherever you go; by foot, by car, by train, by plane; no matter where you intend to ply your trade, and no matter the age or levels of ability and fitness of your client base.

Those two padded leather mitts represent a myriad of ways in which you can challenge, test, motivate and progress every type of client or pupil in the smallest of spaces, with the barest of facilities, in the shortest available time. They are a portable target; a mine of creative ideas; your archetypal flexible friend.

Perhaps you think this is overstating the case... but have faith, because you will come to appreciate the value to the exercise professional of a good pair of focus mitts. Before you can do so, however, you *must* learn how to hold and use them correctly. Far too many trainers can still be seen in gyms, parks and other spaces simply holding up two pads and droning on: 'one, two, one, two' as the bored client slogs away – or, worse still, slapping or punching out with the pads aggressively, regardless of the potential damage to their client's hands, wrists and psyche.

Don't fall into the same traps. Study Part Three of this *Complete Guide*, where a master on the focus pads – former British and European boxing champion, and boxing fitness guru **Clinton McKenzie** – guides you through the dos and don'ts of holding and positioning the mitts, together with the many ways in which you can develop fluency and skill in their use.

Then, when you're sure you have the basics right, start holding the pads for your client's straight shots and combinations. Here is a quick summary of the key points for good pad work:

- Make sure the pads are snug around your wrists, and hold them firmly in place (without a death-like finger-grip).
- For straight shots – which are what you are concentrating on to begin with – hold the pads vertically so they make a straight line with your forearm as your elbows point towards the ground (see figure 11.1).
- Position them just above your shoulder height, and around shoulder-width apart. DO NOT hold the pads in front of your face, ever. If you eventually want to replicate the real position of an opponent's head – which is obviously a single, smaller target – you do it with one pad (see pages 106-7), not with the two pads held close together. It only takes one misjudged punch for you to suffer a world of hurt.
- You need to take up the client's stance, even if it's not the stance you yourself prefer. If they are boxing orthodox, your stance is orthodox and you hold up the left pad for their jab. If they are boxing southpaw, your stance is southpaw and the left pad will be held up for their back hand. At first this can be really confusing. There is only one solution: lots and lots of practice in both stances. *Some* trainers (naming no names) have been known to avoid southpaws

like the plague, even going so far as to coerce their clients into working orthodox although it doesn't suit them. Others embrace southpaws as if they were the future, and try to convert everyone else to the true religion! Neither way is professional, and you will never be properly good on the pads if you can't master the technique on both sides.

- Finally, don't keep both pads in the air all the time. Even if you are calling out the required punches, it's better to raise the appropriate pad for each shot in turn. This is less confusing for your client – although more difficult at first for you – and encourages them to watch carefully and react quickly to what is required, thus

Figure 11.1 Holding the pad correctly – away from the face, elbow pointing down. The mitt makes a straight line with the forearm..

standing them in good stead for faster, more complicated work in the future (see also above – 'Too late, mate!'). Having said that, for the *one-two* and the *three* and *four straight*, you'll keep both pads up, because lifting and lowering them doesn't make sense – it takes too long and interrupts the flow of the combination.

Just as with the punch bag, take time to position your client within appropriate range so that they're neither reaching/lunging from too far out to make contact with the pad(s), nor so close that they have insufficient space in which to punch correctly and effectively.

Some clients may be nervous and feel the need to 'protect' their personal space – this is understandable, because boxing is new to them. In such cases you may find them leaning back with their chin in the air, shoulders tense and legs rigid. Encourage them to relax, bend loosely at the knees and 'sink' gently into the ground, bringing everything down into the balanced, relaxed and grounded stance they have already practised and mastered. Give them time to get used to this new way of working.

By contrast, others may get a little carried away and whack the pads aggressively, pushing *you* backwards and invading *your* personal space! Also understandable: nerves, excitement, enthusiasm, enjoyment, or a need to express pent-up frustration and stress in an appropriate setting. This is all good, and an integral part of boxing fitness. But remind them that to get the most out of their training, control is paramount. If they channel their aggression into shots delivered with the correct technique, the results will be even more satisfying.

For all clients, encourage them to listen carefully to the *sound* their glove makes in contact with the focus pad. If they get it right, a sharp 'crack' will attest to this. You really can hear a difference: punches that lack power or hit the pad at the wrong angle do not generate this kind of noise.

Figure 11.2 Holding the pads for an orthodox client.

INTRODUCING FOOTWORK

After you and your client have practised and are confident with some basic combinations as static drills – with and without a target – introduce some footwork. This is covered in detail in Chapter 8.

In the early days of putting shots and combinations together with footwork, there's an awful lot to think about: a lot for your client to remember, and a great deal for you to keep an eye on. So keep things very simple at first. Remind your student that *boxers rarely punch on the move*. Sometimes it may look as if they are, because elite athletes can be so skilled that offence, defence and footwork flow with apparently seamless transition. But if you watch carefully, you'll notice that shots and combinations are always delivered from a balanced stance, between bursts of footwork that position and re-position the boxer deftly for optimal attack and evasion.

The rhythm you should encourage is thus: punch – *move* – punch – *move* – punch – *move*. Start off with single, straight shots with no target; just stick to watching them shadow box for the time being. Work the jab first, and call the shots out for your client until they're sufficiently well versed in the techniques to think for themselves.

Here's an example: 'Jab! Now move! That's it, in and out, keep that back foot offset – careful never to cross your feet over. A little more bend at the knees… Good, that looks great. Stay relaxed. Shoulders down. Now stop, jab again; double it up – and move!'

Then introduce the cross/back hand. 'Throw a back hand. Don't forget to pivot the rear hip… see how much more power that generates! Snap your hand back into the guard. Now move, keep your elbows in, hands up; I don't want to see that chin, ever. Remember, move in all directions, not just forwards and back. Stop, and give me a one-two. And another. Move… great. Now stand still and shake it out.'

Develop their movement skills slowly, while working the straight shots singly and in combination as part of their shadow boxing, punch bag and focus pad routines. These disciplines are covered in detail in the respective chapters or sections of this *Complete Guide*.

12

TEACHING
// DEFENCE

Of course, footwork is an essential part of a boxer's defence – but it is by no means the only one. It's all very well being able to move their whole body out of range, to avoid getting hit; but if they never stood their ground to 'trade punches' with an opponent, they might never land any scoring blows of their own. So they have to be able to block, ward off (parry), slip, duck, roll under and counter (respond to) an opponent's punches while standing in front of them. This is known in the trade as fighting toe to toe; if the two contestants are standing so close as to be unable to land clean, straight shots at range, it's called fighting on the inside.

Your clients aren't going to get hit during their boxing fitness training, so you don't necessarily have to cover a wide range of defensive skills. But introducing some of a boxer's core defences into their repertoire can lend the workout another dimension – not just in terms of variety (which is always good), but also in terms of movement around the different axes and planes of the body. This is especially useful for core and functional training, covered in more detail in Parts Three and Five.

So this chapter covers those basic defensive manoeuvres that are most useful to the exercise professional teaching non-contact boxing to their clients. It's not within the remit or scope of this *Complete Guide* to cover all the defences; there are no fewer than 11 recognised defences against the jab alone. But if you want to know more, some further references are given in the 'Resources' section.

When teaching the following techniques to your clients, make sure they keep their head down and their guard up. A common defensive fault is to rear backwards, exposing the chin – which is never a good idea in boxing. You can use the focus pads in a range of ways to simulate the shots and combinations you're asking them to avoid: see Part Three for specific advice, and some ideas for effective drills incorporating defence.

DUCKING

This is perhaps the simplest way of evading a punch, and works just like it sounds – the boxer 'sits' by bending the knees; the blow that has been aimed at them misses and passes straight over their head (see also pages 46–7 on the jab to the body and the 'sitting' technique).

Working with your client, you can simulate the attacking jab by simply pushing out your hand or focus pad as if to land the blow. *Obviously*, don't hit them.

When ducking, remind your student to maintain a straight back, as if sitting down into a chair, rather than bending the upper back or at the hips. Make sure they don't squat down too far (it's just further to come up again, and slows the manoeuvre), or look at the floor. The boxing stance should be maintained throughout. Their hands can move slightly upwards in the guard as they duck, to protect a little more of the face and forehead.

Training benefit:

The ducking movement is like a squat in resistance training, strengthening and toning the quadriceps, hamstrings and gluteals as well as burning calories. It can be used to good effect in a number of different boxing fitness drills: some examples are given in Parts Three and Five. Like all the defences covered here, ducking to miss an incoming shot will improve the speed of your clients' reactions and encourage their focus and discipline.

SLIPPING

When 'slipping' an incoming punch, the boxer will rotate their upper body slightly by pivoting the hips and shoulders so that the blow passes harmlessly next to their head. The slip is a small movement; too strong a pivot and it will throw them off balance, inhibiting recovery into the stance.

Note that the guard should be up, the chin down, and the elbows tucked in. Remind your client always to look at you (the 'opponent') rather than allowing their gaze to turn away with the upper body's rotation. Get them to try both the *inside* and the *outside slip*: i.e. slipping inside and outside an incoming jab. So, for two orthodox boxers:

Figure 12.1 Ducking the jab.

Figure 12.2 Slipping outside the jab.

- *The inside slip*: Boxer A throws a jab with their lead (left) hand. Boxer B slips inside the jab by pivoting their hips and shoulders anti-clockwise; the jab passes to the right of their head, over their right shoulder.
- *The outside slip*: Boxer A throws a jab with their lead (left) hand. Boxer B slips outside the jab by pivoting their hips and shoulders clockwise; the jab passes to the left of their head, over their left shoulder (see figure 12.2).

Adjust the instructions accordingly for southpaws. When teaching the slip, you will be Boxer A and simulate the attacking jab with your hand or focus pad.

Training benefit:
The slipping movement is great for working your clients' core muscles – covered in more detail in Part Five. Like all the defences covered here, slipping inside or outside an incoming shot will improve the speed of your clients' reactions and encourage their focus and discipline.

THE PUSH-AWAY
This is a footwork defence, and it does what it says on the tin: the defending boxer uses their front foot to push away from an incoming shot.

As the opponent's attacking shot begins to travel towards them, the boxer simply pushes into the ground with the ball of their lead foot, simultaneously stepping backwards with the rear leg. It's *not* a lean or a 'lay back'; as with all footwork covered in Chapter 8, the front foot must quickly follow the back, so that the stance is regained. The attacking shot then falls short of its target.

When practising this with your client, throw a dummy jab or push your focus pad out to simulate

Figure 12.3 The push-away moves the boxer out of range of the attacking jab.

an attacking shot. Your client has to react quickly with the push-away. To add complexity, you can then instruct them to step back in and *counter* – respond – with a jab, or a one-two, of their own.

Training benefit:

This is all about good reactions: the push-away must be quick and definite. Repeated as a drill (for example, on the focus pads: ask them for a jab; counter with a feint or dummy shot of your own, from which they must push away; and then get them to advance again for a one-two – repeated, say 3 x 10 times) it becomes effective cardio work as well as demanding serious coordination and focus.

'BOBBING AND WEAVING' – OR ROLLING UNDER A PUNCH

Termed 'bobbing and weaving' in professional boxing, this defence combines a slip and a duck (see above) with a rolling movement under the incoming shot. It can take a little while to get the hang of the technique, so encourage your client to practise hard – preferably in front of a full-length mirror so they can see what they're doing.

To teach the technique, stand opposite your client and throw out a dummy jab. Instruct them to slip to one side of the shot or the other (it doesn't matter which for now), at the same time bending at the knees with a straight back as if ducking (see figure 12.4a). They then 'roll' their upper body underneath your dummy shot (see 12.4b), coming back up on the other side of your outstretched arm by extending the knees to return to the stance (see 12.4c). Throughout, they must

(a)

(b)

(c)

Figure 12.4 Rolling inside the jab.

keep their guard up, their elbows and chin tucked in, and their eyes looking at you.

Stress that all the movements involved in this defence are small, swift and slight. You'll find that many clients are tempted to do a great, dramatic roll, bending at the hips, looking down and swinging the whole of their upper body round in a big circle. Ask them: When would a boxer trying to evade a blow to the head have the time, balance or inclination for such a defence? Instead, emphasise that only the knees and a small 'swinging' motion at the midriff actually achieve the roll. It can help to describe the movement as drawing the letter 'c' (a small 'c', not a capital!) in the air with the upper body.

Your client can roll either inside or outside the jab, as follows. In the description, you are facing each other, both standing orthodox. You, the trainer, are Boxer A; adjust the instructions accordingly for a southpaw client:

• *Rolling inside the jab*: Boxer A throws a jab with their lead (left) hand. Boxer B slips inside (to the(ir) left of) the jab by pivoting their hips and shoulders anti-clockwise; at the same time they duck by bending the knees slightly with a straight back, and roll their upper body quickly underneath A's outstretched jabbing arm, coming up on the(ir) right of A's arm by extending the knees to recover the stance.

• *Rolling outside the jab*: Boxer A throws a jab with their lead (left) hand. Boxer B slips outside (to the(ir) right of) the jab by pivoting their hips and shoulders clockwise; at the same time they duck by bending the knees slightly with a straight back, and roll their upper body quickly underneath A's outstretched jabbing arm, coming up on the(ir) left of A's arm by extending their knees to recover the stance.

Training benefit:

This is a great technique for improving your clients' core strength, since it engages the obliques and abdominals as well as encouraging flexibility and stability in the lower back. The ducking element further serves to strengthen and tone the quadriceps, hamstrings and gluteals. As a drill, repeated by rolling from one side to the other like a pendulum, it is seriously hard work! And, along with all the defences covered here, rolling inside or outside a dummy attacking shot will improve the speed of students' reactions while encouraging focus and concentration.

THE ELBOW BLOCK

As we've said already, the target area for a boxer's scoring shots is not just their opponent's head; it also includes the front of their body, from the shoulders to just above the 'belt' (an imaginary line drawn from hip to hip above the navel).

This defence – the *elbow block* – is designed specifically to defend against body shots, which, correctly delivered, are not just legal scoring punches but can also be very hurtful and debilitating. Your boxing fitness clients don't need to worry about the pain, but in learning how to protect their body against imaginary attacks, they can add an extra movement dimension to their workouts.

Body shots can be straight punches delivered from the lead or the back hand; they can also be hooks or uppercuts delivered at varying angles and from different positions. If a boxer's guard is nice and tight, with the elbows tucked closely into the torso, a good deal of their body is already protected from direct shots thrown from the front. So, in order to make contact, their opponent has to look for openings below

Figure 12.5 Preparing to use the elbows to block body shots, as a defence drill.

or round the side of the elbows – always making sure they don't stray into illegal territory such as the kidneys or 'low blows'.

Keeping things simple with straight shots, to defend against a cross/back hand to the body, your client will simply move their lead elbow across the target area – literally, to cover the targeted part of their body and block the attacking shot. Because the elbow must always stay close to the body in the guard, the defence necessitates a slight rotation of the upper body to achieve the movement: clockwise for orthodox, anti-clockwise for southpaw.

To defend against a jab to the body, it will be the rear elbow that will block the shot, with the upper body moving in the other direction.

If you are training your client on the focus pads, you can simulate an attack to the body by pushing out the rear or lead pad in the requisite direction – perhaps calling out 'block' or 'elbow' to indicate the defence you're looking for.

Training benefit:

This is another movement that works and strengthens the core muscles: great for the waistline.

An effective drill is to get the client performing alternate-side elbow blocks repeatedly, so they are effectively rotating their upper body *left-right-left-right*. You can tap their elbows with the pads at varying speeds – sharpening their focus, coordination and reaction times.

COUNTERPUNCHING

Countering an opponent's shots just means 'answering' them – punching back in response. You look for openings created by your opponent's attack. A simple example is as follows:

- Boxer A throws a jab. Boxer B defends – perhaps, say, with a deft inside slip (see pages 69–70). Having delivered the jab, of necessity Boxer A has to retract his/her lead hand back into the guard, before following up with another punch or some footwork to move themselves into another position. If Boxer B is lightning-quick, at the same time as A is completing the jab, B responds with a punch of his/her own – making the most of any small window of opportunity created by A's attack.
- Remember: if A's technique is good, their jab hand will return along the same line as it was delivered, snapping back into the guard... so B may have no success landing a return jab. They might do better to follow their own slip with a hook to A's head or body.

It will be evident even from this example that counterpunching is a skill in itself, requiring excellent reflexes, strategic intelligence, accurate punching and above-average hand speed. For your boxing fitness clients, it can make shadow boxing in particular more fun and creative as they imagine what shots and combinations may be coming their way from a skilled opponent.

Encourage them, while watching their shadow boxing routine, to respond to such imaginary offensives with a mixture of footwork, different defences (as covered in this chapter) and single or combination counters. Let them work for themselves, with you just correcting the odd technical fault which may creep in, or calling out some suggestions: 'Jab! Again! Good, now move... they're coming back at you with a double jab back hand, so roll underneath the cross and then throw four straight of your own – *one-two-one-two*, nice and quick. That's great! Push away, now step back in for your double jab... and finish with a killer knockout!'

There are plenty of suggestions for incorporating defences and counters in your clients' shadow boxing, punch bag and focus pad work in the following pages. Try these, or invent your own. Remember: you're the boss! The only limit to your boxing fitness repertoire is your clients' safety, and your own creative imagination.

TEACHING SHADOW BOXING, BAG WORK AND SKIPPING

13

TEACHING SHADOW BOXING

Shadow boxing is hard to teach. By definition it is a solitary activity, as the boxer pits him- or herself against an imaginary opponent, and moves around as if 'the two of them' were actually competing in the ring. The best shadow boxing combines all of the techniques covered so far in this *Complete Guide*: working from the correct stance with their guard up, the practitioner throws individual shots as well as punches in combination, all the while using a good range of defences against potential counters and employing deft, balanced footwork to move in and out of range. And they do this using their imagination and creativity – since there is, in fact, no one else there; they are literally 'boxing at shadows'.

Frankly, until you get used to shadow boxing and are able to focus on the task in hand, fully understanding its benefits, it can make you feel a bit stupid. You need to be aware of this, so that you can empathise with and encourage your clients when they are starting out.

EXPLAIN THE BENEFITS

Before you tackle shadow boxing with your clients, explain to them why it is an important part of their boxing fitness programme. Boxers will always do a

'The first time I tried shadow boxing I felt like a right idiot. I kept expecting someone to shout, "The other guy has left the ring, mate!" But I persevered and now it's second nature. Shadow boxing prepares my muscles and my mind for the session ahead. It gets me in the zone.' (Amateur boxer)

number of rounds of shadow boxing at the start of their workouts, or prior to competitive bouts, for the following reasons:

- It functions as a dynamic warm-up.
- It serves to practise and fine-tune their core skills, developing 'muscle memory' (see page 30) and building a repertoire of fluid, balanced boxing techniques.
- It helps them to focus, shutting out extraneous noise and distractions and channelling nervous energy.
- It enables them to try out various tactics for dealing with a sparring partner or opponent.
- It is hard, aerobic work, and therefore a great conditioning tool.

Once your clients appreciate the range of benefits inherent in shadow boxing, they will probably be happy to give it a go. But that doesn't mean they know what to do, so you can't just say, 'Right, let's have three rounds of shadow boxing!' You need to give them some structure and guidance.

PROVIDE ENCOURAGEMENT AND FEEDBACK

If you have followed the advice given so far in this section of the book, your clients will already have started boxing while on the move – practising their shots, combinations and defences with footwork. This, of course, is the essence of shadow boxing: they're already doing it. Your role as the trainer is to:

- *Watch.* Don't just tell your client to go off and shadow box; it's not helpful or professional. They are likely to feel self-conscious, especially if there are other people around, so take them into as private a space as the venue affords and make sure they feel your presence and encouragement throughout. (In a class or group situation, watch and lead the shadow boxing from the front: more suggestions for group training are given on pages 140–2.)
- *Provide a structure.* Time your client's shadow boxing intervals. Depending on their fitness level, you may choose to limit these to, say, 30 seconds of work (a 30-second 'round') and one minute's rest, repeated an appropriate number of times. Then build this up as the client becomes aerobically fitter and technically more proficient. Don't increase the work intervals to more than three minutes, and always allow a full minute's rest between each – replicating the minute's recovery given to a boxer between rounds in a bout.

- *Make suggestions.* Again, these will depend on the stage your client is at in their programme. For a novice, you could begin very simply with the jab. Time them over 30 seconds, giving instructions along these lines: 'OK, jab. And again. Good, nice and relaxed, just throw out the jabs as you feel them. Great. Move around between the shots, changing directions. Now double it up – double jab, and again, and – move. Keep your hands up and your chin down, let's see a bit of head movement, try and imagine the counters coming your way. Duck, good, jab and move…' When they are confi-

example combinations with some motivational comments. 'Come on, like this! *One-two-one-two-one-two*… nice and fast, let's see *you* do it now – great! And again!' This not only shows that you're engaged, it can also really boost their confidence and give them the motivation to try harder.

- *Gradually build things up.* As with all fitness training, you can build on the basics by (a) increasing the duration of the work intervals; and/or (b) upping the pace of their efforts. In other sporting disciplines you have the additional option of reducing the rest/recovery period, but as has already been stressed elsewhere in this book, this is not advisable in boxing. Keep to the minute's rest. You can always add in more, and more complex, combinations to keep things fresh and challenging.

- *Have a laugh.* Make shadow boxing fun. If you do, your client will stop worrying about how they look or what other people think, and just get on with it.

RECOMMEND LOTS OF PRACTICE

Like any skill, shadow boxing quickly improves with practice. Suggest to your client that they have a go at home, between sessions – perhaps in front of a full-length mirror, if they have one and can find sufficient space to move around. They can then use their own reflection as an 'opponent', judging the angles and positioning of their shots, while checking that their guard is up, their chin tucked down and so on.

Remind them to time their rounds, even when you're not there. This will give them a defined target for starting and completing their efforts; also, when they report back to you on what they've managed, this enables you to establish

dent with this, introduce the cross/back hand: 'Now throw a big straight right *[or left, depending on their stance]*, let's see a good strong pivot with that rear hip. Great, but roll out of the punch, don't just stand and admire it! Back on the jab, double it…' How you guide them is up to you; just make sure you do.

- *Teach by example.* As well as watching, encouraging and helping to structure your client's shadow boxing efforts, demonstrate. Use that tried-and-tested combination of show-and-tell. You don't have to get them slavishly copying your every move; simply throw in a few progressive targets as they work through their programme.

Finally, encourage them not to give up. If they are finding the going tough, suggest ways in which they can pace themselves. They might set small, measurable goals such as running through each of the combinations, learned during the previous session, five or ten times, with a few seconds' rest and a 'shake-out' before repeating. This will help focus their minds on something other than their fatigue or anxiety about technique, and make the time pass quicker.

The training programmes set out on pages 156–62 of this *Complete Guide* include more suggestions for incorporating shadow boxing in your clients' workouts.

TEACHING BAG WORK

Depending on your training venue, you may or may not be able to incorporate punch bag work into your clients' sessions. As was discussed in Part One, increasing numbers of health clubs, fitness gyms and schools are recognising the physical and therapeutic value of hitting a heavy bag, and are providing basic models for their clients' or pupils' use – although you are unlikely to find the more specialised models, such as the uppercut or angle bags, anywhere outside a boxing club.

If you have the use of a punch bag, all well and good; if not, this is not a deal-breaker, since you can replicate the benefits of bag work via the other boxing fitness disciplines – perhaps combined with weight training or circuits (see pages 156–62 for specific workout and programme suggestions).

VARY AND TAILOR THE WORK

In general, boxers use the punch bag to build stamina and power; to improve their speed, reaction time and reflexes; and to enhance their technical skills – not only in the punches and combinations, but also in footwork and defence. You can include rounds of punch bag work in your clients' sessions as general fitness training, or tailor their bag work to achieve particular fitness gains. For example:

- To improve their speed, get them to throw shots and combinations quickly, with bursts of fast footwork around the bag.
- To build their stamina/muscular endurance, structure their rounds to include more continuous shots and combinations, with less 'breathing space' between each work effort – but always allow a full minute's recovery between rounds.
- To increase strength/power, include more single shots delivered with technical accuracy to generate as much power as possible: e.g. the cross/back hand, delivered repeatedly with strong pivot of the hips and torso.
- To enhance agility, balance and coordination, concentrate on deft footwork and defence techniques in response to the bag's movements.

If you are lucky enough to have access to different types of punch bag, you can use these to further fine-tune your clients' work. For strength and power, you might have them working on the heaviest bag available, so that it hardly moves in response to their shots. (Alternatively, of course, you can simply hold a lighter bag against your torso as they hit it.) For agility and balance you might get them to work on a double-end bag, which is fixed to both floor and ceiling with elastic, and has a rapid rebound that is hard to predict. This is great for their reflexes, but also develops core strength and stability by demanding lots of lateral, evasive movements of the head, shoulders and torso.

Even if you are limited to straight shots and combinations on a basic punch bag, you can get your clients to work at different levels – literally, as well as figuratively. Ask them to imagine a very tall 'opponent', so they have to punch higher than their own shoulder-level to make contact with the jab; or a smaller guy so they have to punch down or work in a semi-squat.

And don't forget the body shots! A good exercise is as follows:

- Duck
- Throw a combination to the 'body' of the bag
- Rise up into the stance
- Throw the same combination to the 'head'
- Duck
- Repeat – any number of times over a set period with short rests built in

This is hard work, involving all the large muscle groups, the core, and the cardiorespiratory system. Get your clients to try it, or think up your own imaginative drills. The important thing is that their punch bag workouts remain fresh and challenging rather than becoming monotonous.

SOME SAFETY CONSIDERATIONS

When using the punch bag, ensure that your client wears hand-wraps beneath good-quality boxing gloves. Don't let them work the bag in weight-training gloves, in their hand-wraps alone, or with bare hands. Some people think this will 'toughen them up', but however authentic it may make them feel, they are at serious risk of damaging their hands. Rocky didn't really use his bare hands on frozen carcasses hanging in the abattoir, folks.

Even with wraps and gloves on, the skin on your clients' knuckles may become sore due to the repeated, chafing contact of leather on leather. If mild redness is aggravated until the skin is broken, this can take a long time to heal and will prohibit punch bag *and* focus pad work for some time – which is frustrating for everyone. After a while, mild callouses may form over your clients' knuckles, protecting them. Until then, keep an eye on their hands and safeguard their everyday activities, as well as the future of their boxing training.

Finally, remind your client that *the bag will move when they hit it*. This is not as stupid as it sounds. In no other boxing fitness discipline does the equipment 'bite back' – unless, of course, you count your focus pads as you push them out to elicit a particular defence or counter. Depending on the type of bag, and its weight, the amount of return movement your client will get in response to a shot or combination varies significantly. Make sure *you* know what to expect; try out any new equipment for yourself before letting anyone else loose on it. And explain to your client that having to move their head, shoulders, torso and feet to get out of the way of a swaying punch bag is at least as important as hitting it in the first place – for all the reasons given above.

ACTIVELY ENGAGE IN THEIR BAG WORK

As an exercise professional, you already know that active engagement in a client's training – whatever form it takes – is of paramount importance. Health and fitness is a service industry, and clients are paying for experienced, knowledgeable, empathetic guidance and feedback. They have the right to expect your full interaction throughout their

sessions, and even between them, should they need additional support.

So, as with shadow boxing (see above) and skipping (see below), engage with your clients as they work on the heavy bag. Too many trainers can still be seen telling people to 'go off and do six rounds', as they themselves have a chat with a colleague or talk on their mobile phone. Frankly, your client could do that kind of training all by themselves; why would they shell out for the privilege? Boxing fitness should be hard work for you, as well as for your students, and learning the best ways in which to encourage and motivate them is

a skill in itself. Here are some tips for helping your clients through their punch bag sessions.

• Develop the ability to stand close to them as they work the bag, without getting in the way – either of them, or of the equipment. Have you ever considered how you *don't* notice the referee during an elite boxing contest? Referees undergo any number of training courses and exams just to become that good at not getting in the way of the action (and not getting punched by mistake), while placing themselves in the best position to see what's going on. Concentrate on what your client is doing, and try to anticipate what's coming next. Move accordingly, using your own footwork skills.

- Help your client structure their rounds on the bag, either by setting specific tasks beforehand, or by making suggestions as they work (or both). If they are struggling, cardio-wise, encourage them to step back, shake it out, breathe – they really do forget, sometimes – and get back on the jab: 'Come on, only 30 seconds left! You're doing really well. Pace yourself, focus on the jab. Double it. And move – good.' Yell at them occasionally! Put some of yourself into the session: you'd be surprised how motivational this can be for people, compared to being left solo with only their pain, sweat and fatigue for company.

- Obviously, as well as keeping an eye on your client's state of mind and body throughout each round, you should correct any technical faults that may occur. It's especially important that their wrists remain strong as they punch the bag, to avoid injury: refer to Chapters 9 and 11 if you need to recap on the key teaching points for straight shots and combinations. But achieve a balance between fault-correction and passive observation – a balance that allows the client's work to flow. As with the other boxing fitness disciplines, if you constantly pick up on each little error, you will quickly find they become disheartened.

- Build up their efforts with measurable progression. Even if they have good basic fitness, they will find bag work tough-going – it *is* and *should be* tough-going. Aim initially for, say, 15- or 30-second effort intervals with short breathers in between, always remembering to include a full minute's recovery between

rounds. Gradually increase the intensity, with the ultimate objective of maintaining a good-paced workout over three minutes. This may take some weeks, so make sure you keep a record of their achievements. It's very rewarding for both of you to see those effort-intervals increase, and the rounds adding up.

The training programmes set out on pages 156–62 of this *Complete Guide* include more specific suggestions for incorporating punch bag work in your clients' sessions.

TEACHING SKIPPING

Skipping is not a 'girl thing', no matter how your macho clients or disaffected schoolboys may protest otherwise. Rope work is an integral part of boxing training. It should be apparent by now that there are sound physiological and psychological bases underlying every element in a boxer's training regime, and skipping is no exception. It builds endurance, encourages focus and concentration, and plays an essential role in developing balance, coordination and agility. Competitive boxing requires all these skills for the effective delivery of punches and combinations, and for dextrous footwork. And boxing fitness relies on skipping as one of its most flexible disciplines: together with shadow boxing and focus pads, it can be done anywhere.

Like shadow boxing, skipping is not easy to teach if your client has never done it before. The best thing is to give them a rope and a few fundamental pointers – see below – and then let them have a go. Reassure them that everyone finds skipping tricky and frustrating at first, but it really does pay to persevere. Once they've become proficient with the basics (and they *will*), there are many different ways of using the rope to improve both their fitness and their boxing.

SIMPLE CONSIDERATIONS

Before you start, remember the advice given in Chapter 4 and make sure there is sufficient space for full turns of the rope. This means space both around your client, and above them. No one is going to thank you if, during your initial demonstration, you take out an expensive chandelier or behead the prize roses on the patio.

It may seem glaringly obvious, but taller clients require more room around them, as well as more rope. You're likely to find that a standard speed rope tends to be too long, rather than too short, for the majority of people, and this is an easy problem to address: simply tie the requisite number of knots in each end. In terms of ideal length, you can check this by getting your client to stand on the middle of the rope while holding the ends; the handles should reach just up to their underarm. It's personal, though: some people prefer their rope longer, and some shorter, so you can pretty much leave it up to them to experiment and find out what suits them best.

For your clients' health and safety it is important that they skip on a suitable surface. Too hard, and they may experience stress injuries to their feet, shins, knees, hips and even lower back, while on an irregular floor there may be trip hazards. In the garden or park, spongy ground or long grass will make the going very tricky and interrupt their rhythm. If possible choose a smooth, shock-absorbing surface such as a wooden 'sprung' floor, or use a gym mat (one that won't slip from under them as they move). If your training venue is outside, you might find a running track or a racket-ball court with a forgiving surface.

Bear in mind, too, that if your client is very heavy, skipping will cause particular strain on their joints and they are likely to find the activity especially tough. In such cases you may want to limit the amount of rope work they do, at least until their weight starts to come down, or even omit it altogether – compensating by building in more shadow boxing, punch bag work and/or focus pad drills.

Advise all your clients to wear a comfortable, supportive pair of trainers for their rope work. Boxing boots are great for shadow boxing, punch bag and focus pad work, but may not provide sufficient cushioning for skipping, which is an impact activity.

FIRST SHOW THEM HOW

As has been mentioned many times in this book already, don't try to teach your client something you can't do yourself: make sure first that you have already mastered the rudimentary skill. With skipping in particular, it will really help if you give a quick initial demonstration, as slowly as you can. Stick to basic double-footed skipping in the early days (see below), and talk your client or pupils through the main teaching points before they have a go.

If you trip a few times as you are showing them, that's OK: have a laugh about it. Everyone messes it up, even the most experienced boxers, and this will encourage novices as they are stumbling around and detangling their rope amid a lot of swear words. Seeing you getting it wrong, sorting yourself out and then trying again actually gives them the best possible message: *keep on going*.

THE KEY TEACHING POINTS

When you've shown them how (or how not!) to skip, run through the key teaching points as follows:

- They should stand with good posture, holding one end of the rope in each hand with the mid-section of the rope resting on the floor behind their feet.
- They then swing the rope forwards over their head, using a small circular movement of hands and forearms. This movement is initiated from the elbows, which remain close to the body; it is not a big rotation generated by the shoulders.
- As the rope descends in front of them and reaches the floor, they attempt a small, double-footed jump over it. Stress to your client that they don't need to jump as high as they might think! Most inexperienced skippers will overcompensate by bending their knees and almost doing a tuck jump to clear the rope. In fact, if you watch boxers skipping, their legs remain almost straight and there is hardly any space visible between their feet and the floor – the rope merely skimming along its surface.
- If the rope clears their feet, encourage the client to keep its momentum going with a continued motion of their hands and forearms, so that it carries on in a circle – back over their head and down again towards the floor. They then jump again… and they are officially skipping. (If the rope doesn't clear their feet, simply instruct them to return to the starting position and try again. And again.)

Expect some initial frustration, and focus on the positive: 'That's great! Last week you managed between three and ten rotations of the rope at any one time; today, you've skipped for 30 seconds without tripping. Let's do a total of six rounds this session: 30 seconds on and a minute off. We've made real progress.'

When your client or pupils have mastered the basic, two-footed technique, encourage them to have a go at some different skipping styles. Remind them that even though they may be stop-starting their way through the effort-intervals you set for them, they are still improving their fitness. They are in constant motion, with their heart rate raised and their lungs and muscles working hard over a sustained period. The point isn't being able to do it; it's continuing to try.

SOME DIFFERENT SKIPPING TECHNIQUES

- *Running in place.* This is a natural progression from the small, double-footed jumps, but some clients find that they prefer it from the outset. The technique is just as it sounds: remaining stationary (i.e. without travelling as they 'run' – see below), they lift alternate knees with each turn of the rope as if they were running in an exaggerated way. With each knee lift – left, right, left, right – the rope makes one full rotation.
- *Travelling with the rope.* This can be done with either technique – double-footed jumps or 'running' (high, alternating knee-lifts). The client simply moves along the floor as they skip. They can travel forwards, backwards and from side to side; work the perimeter of an imaginary square; or make up their own shapes.
- *One-footed skipping.* First, they get into their rhythm with some double-footed jumps. When they are skipping fluidly, they then pick one knee up and hold it there, continuing to turn the rope so that they are effectively hopping on one leg. Get them to perform several rotations on that side before swapping to the other. If they become confident with this, they could try 'travelling' (see above) while they hop.

Figure 13.1 Running in place.

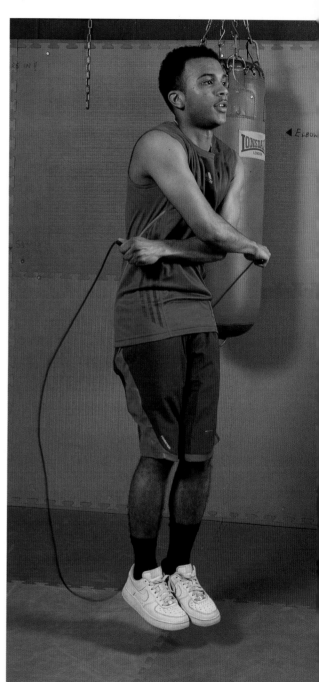

Figure 13.2 Cross-overs.

- *Double-unders*. Straying into impressive territory! If your client really wants to emulate a boxer, suggest they try making two turns of the rope for every one double-footed jump. Explain that in order to succeed with this technique, they will need to jump higher and spin the rope much faster. Suggest that they start by adding in just a few double-unders during the course of a round of basic skipping: it's surprising how challenging this is. If they work on the transition between the double-unders and the basic skipping rhythm, in time they will develop the ability to perform several double-unders consecutively – or even do a whole minute without stopping. Then, they can try double-unders on one leg...

- *Cross-overs*. This technique is very advanced. As they skip, they cross their arms at the elbows on the downward arc of the rope. They then jump through the loop of the rope that forms in front of their body, uncrossing the arms on the next downward swing – and repeat. If they can do this, they are very good at skipping, and probably don't need you!! But if they still want a challenge, they could try all of the above...

- *... skipping backwards*.

3

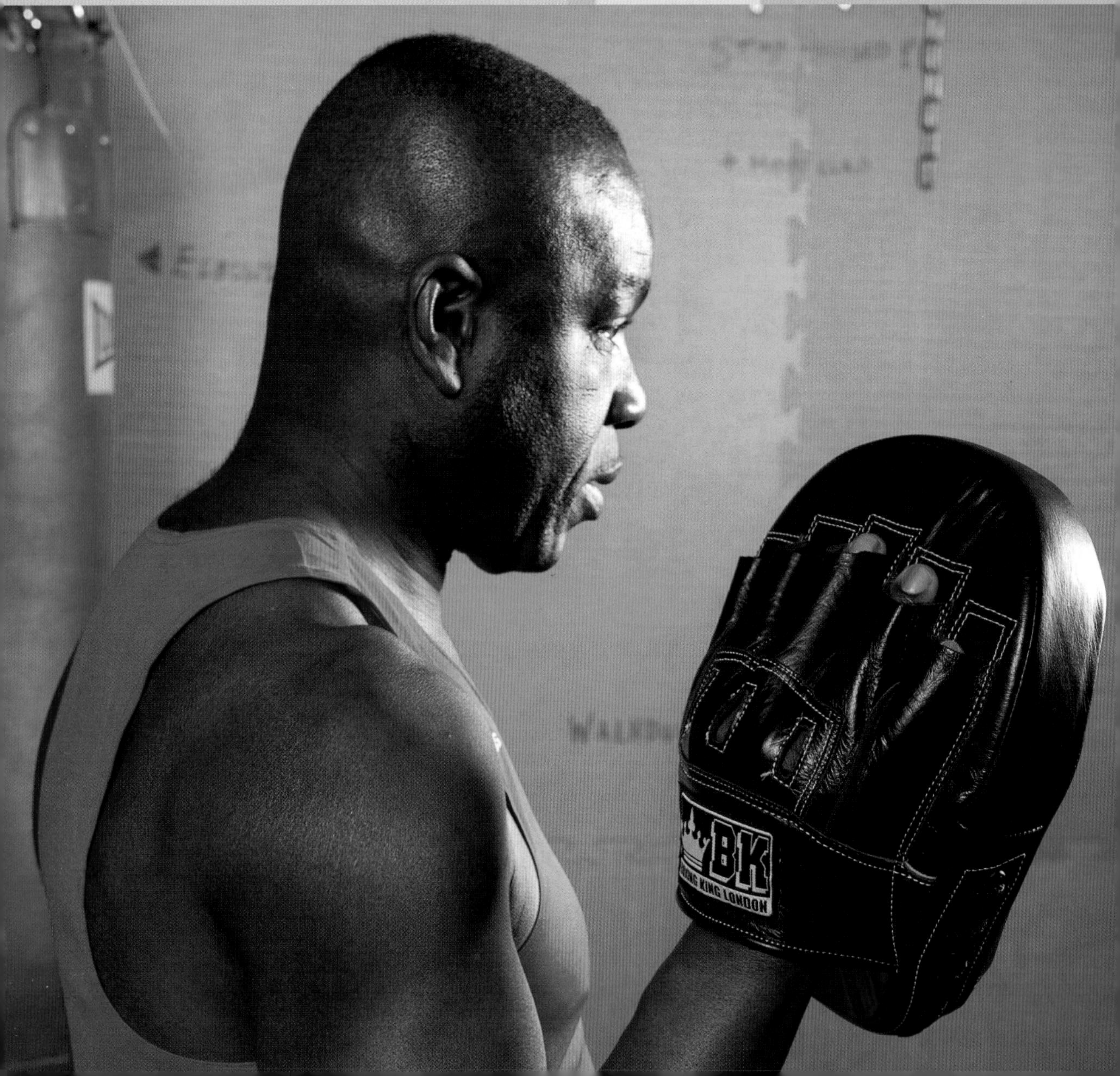

PART THREE

USING THE FOCUS PADS (OR GLOVE-AND-PAD WORK)

This section of the book is dedicated to the focus pads – arguably your most important tool for effective boxing fitness training. Here, **Clinton McKenzie**, former Olympian and British and European champion, clearly identifies the particular benefits of glove-and-pad work to the exercise professional.

'As one of the first female professional boxers in the UK, I've worked on the focus pads with many trainers around the country – over a period of about 10 years. Of all of them, even at the most famous gyms, Clinton McKenzie is by far the best. Clinton always knows how hard to push me, so that my training is fully effective but never beyond what I'm able to achieve, and appropriate to the stage I'm at as I prepare for a bout. I've watched Clinton work with literally thousands of children, men and women – boxers and fitness clients – and he has an instinct for helping them enjoy themselves hugely while getting better and fitter, almost without realising it. His advice is like gold-dust for the exercise professional: take it, and enjoy your boxing training!'
(Female professional boxer, London)

THE BENEFITS OF FOCUS PAD WORK

14

BENEFITS FOR THE TRAINER

OPPORTUNITIES FOR INDIVIDUAL ASSESSMENT/DEVELOPMENT

Clinton says: As a trainer, using the focus pads gives you a really good insight into the current skills and abilities of your clients. Sometimes – especially in a group or class environment – it's hard to assess each person's progress. I find that working one-on-one with a client or youngster on the pads, even over a single round, can high-light not just their level of cardiovascular fitness,

but also their technical strengths as well as the weaker points you need to help them with during their workouts, and over the course of their whole programme.

THE CLOSEST YOU CAN GET TO REAL BOXING: SKILL AND HARD WORK!

Clinton says: Of all the different disciplines in boxing fitness training – shadow boxing, punch bag work, skipping – I find that the pads provide the best situation for really pushing your clients. It's the closest you can get to sparring, imitating the demands of actual boxing without the contact. So if they can get fit enough to cope with a signifi-cant number of rounds on the focus pads, they're approaching the fitness standards needed in competitive boxing. And if they can hit the pads accurately, with power, using a variety of shots and combinations, moving well and covering up, I can truly say to someone: you'd hold your own over a few rounds in the ring, mate! Measuring themselves against this is both a great incentive, and a genuine boost to their morale – which in turn serves you well, because you get to keep your clients. And you get to keep them in a progressive, engaged, enjoyable way. They always want more on the focus pads.

I've found this particularly useful with school children: the younger ones, who can get over-excited when left to their own devices; and the older ones, who need to be pushed beyond their comfort zone and to forget about acting 'cool'.

MOST EFFECTIVE FOR TECHNICAL DEVELOPMENT

Clinton says: Some shots and combinations are very awkward to perform on the punch bag – the hooks, and even more so the uppercuts. There are specialised bags available for practising these, but even so it can be hard for inexperienced clients to achieve the correct angle. Even slight errors can result in sore knuckles, hands and wrists. But you don't want to avoid the bent-arm punches altogether, because first, you are teaching your students to box, even without the contact; and second, using just the straight shots and combinations can get

DEVELOPS FOCUS AND CONCENTRATION

Clinton says: The pads are a small target; they're a moving target; and they're a target that can be held in almost endless positions and at almost any angle. When you, the trainer, get really good at using them, you can challenge your clients and the youngsters almost without them realising it. You ask them for what may seem like the same old combination, but actually hold the pads lower, or wider, or at a tighter angle than they're used to. They then have to respond… and this is a learning process. They really have to concentrate, because you are the boss: you're the one asking them to follow specific directions – in contrast to, say, shadow boxing, when they are free to make up their own routines and work at their own pace.

dull after a while, as well as limiting fitness gains such as core strength and stability.

As I said above, a skilled trainer can use the focus pads at all positions and angles, for any type of client. One of my regulars is literally a giant – a really big guy, who teaches basketball at a local school. He could never practise uppercuts on a punch bag! But because I know how to do it and am strong and experienced, I hold the pads horizontally, high enough above my head for him to do so. In the right hands the focus pads can address any boxing technique.

HIGHLY FLEXIBLE

Clinton says: Last but not least, the focus pads are probably the most flexible tool at a trainer's disposal. You can introduce glove-and-pad work very early in someone's training, straight after you've taught them correct stance, basic footwork and the straight shots – the jab and the cross. This means you can quickly communicate the exciting 'feel' of boxing to your clients, keeping them motivated, engaged and coming back for more. And, as has been stressed elsewhere in this book, you can use the pads anywhere. When my gym is busy I have trainers finding a quiet corner, just a few feet of space, in which to work people out – hard! The pads themselves don't cost much, and all your client needs is a pair of hand-wraps and some gloves for you both to be in business.

BENEFITS FOR THE CLIENT/ PUPIL

WHAT'S GOOD FOR THE TRAINER...

Clinton says: It makes sense that what's good for you is also good for your clients. As we've said

above, glove-and-pad work is low-cost, flexible, and an excellent way for the instructor both to progress and to assess people's fitness levels and boxing techniques. If we look at each of these benefits to the trainer, we see that they all transfer directly to the client: (a) the workout is low-cost: the client faces minimal outlay on equipment and gym fees, because the training is (b) flexible, so they can train almost anywhere – at home, in the park, in the garden, in a school hall – and even if they only have a little time. And (c) because you are able to assess and progress your clients easily on the pads, they (and you) quickly see improvements, so you all keep your motivation to continue. It's win-win.

TAILOR-MADE RESULTS

Clinton says: Of course, the best benefit to the client is that focus pad work gets visible results – and those results can be specifically tailored to what people want to achieve. In my experience, most of your boxing fitness clients will come to you looking to lose weight/tone up: this will be their main reason for exercising. If they do regular sessions on the focus pads and are eating sensibly – see Part Four of this book for some clear advice on diet and health – then success is bound to follow. Adding in some or all of the other boxing fitness elements, like shadow boxing, skipping and bag work, will further challenge their heart, lungs and muscles in new ways.

A GREAT 'LEVELLER'

Clinton says: As long as you are proficient on the pads, in the space of just a few minutes – seconds, even – you can significantly increase someone's heart rate and fatigue their muscles. This means the training will never get 'old' for your clients, even if they are young and very fit (and you, the slightly older exercise professional, don't fancy going on a training run with them!). Here's an example of how: get your student to punch the pads *jab-cross-jab-cross* repeatedly and fluently. *One-two-one-two-one-two*. Maybe they can cope fine with that, over several minutes, and they're looking at you, as if to say: 'Yeah?' OK – now get them to do the same thing, but 'advance' on them as they punch, slowly moving forwards so they have to use footwork to retreat, all the while still throwing the combinations. Do this right the way across the park or the school hall: it is unexpectedly tiring! You can very quickly take an energetic kid from 'cocky' to panting, heaving and blissfully quiet… and yet they will come back for more next week because they appreciate the challenge.

DYNAMIC, FUN AND TECHNICALLY AND PHYSICALLY CHALLENGING

Clinton says: Plenty of people from all walks of life are interested in learning how to box, even if they never want to step into a ring. Who can blame them for that? At the risk of stating the obvious, it hurts when someone hits you. But that doesn't mean they should be denied the technical challenge of learning a new skill – and this applies to women just as much as men. One of the things London 2012 taught us all is that women really can box! So get a pair of gloves on your lady clients and let them have a go on the pads. There's always something to improve on, always a breakthrough just around the corner. If you can keep that 'feel' in your glove-and-pad sessions, moving around, mixing up the combinations, applying the pressure in a fun, non-aggressive way, your clients will enjoy every workout.

HOW TO HOLD THE FOCUS PADS – AND HOW NOT TO!

15

The work you do on the focus pads will depend on your experience. If you have never boxed yourself, and this is all new to you, don't try to run before you can walk. By following the advice given in the first two parts of this book, you will have first learned how to deliver and then to teach a jab, followed by a cross/back hand and so on, progressively and simultaneously developing your boxing techniques and teaching ability. Do the same for the focus pads. Be logical.

THE GOLDEN RULE OF FOCUS PAD WORK!

Learn first how to receive a jab and a cross/back hand from clients working out of both the orthodox and the southpaw stance. Remember that you must adopt the same stance as them, and don't be tempted to put off working out of your non-preferred stance. The sooner you make yourself do it, however awkward, the sooner it will become second nature and you will be able easily to switch between stances without even thinking about it. That day will come: be patient and work hard at it.

The basic principle of pad work is actually very simple. You are standing opposite your client, both of you face to face, in the same stance. Here is the golden rule:

If you are both standing orthodox, the client will jab with their left hand and you will receive their jab with your left focus pad. Their cross/back hand will come from their right glove to your right focus pad.

If you are both standing southpaw, the client will jab with their right hand and you will receive their jab with your right focus pad. Their cross/back hand will come from their left glove to your left focus pad.

Simple! Of course it sounds easy, written like this; but when you begin working, you will really appreciate why this *Complete Guide* has stressed throughout how important it is that you learn to box. If you are comfortable with your own boxing techniques, the focus pad work will be much, much easier right from the outset; you will know instinctively what to expect and how to move in response.

If you both adhere to this golden rule – *left glove to left pad, right glove to right pad* – without fail; and if your client also remembers what you have drummed into them since their first-ever boxing fitness session – *always jab with the*

Figure 15.1 Left glove to left pad (a); right glove to right pad (b).

front (lead) hand – then nothing can go badly wrong. Honestly.

Use the pads for the straight shots and combinations until you and your client are both happy and confident to move on. Don't start out with a heavy hitter; begin your focus pad work with someone of roughly your own height (see below) and of manageable strength.

In this same spirit of starting at grassroots level and working upwards, here are some simple tips for the first time you put on a pair of focus pads. (This advice assumes you have already researched, tried and purchased your own mitts, which fit and feel right, according to the guidance given on pages 15–16.)

A CORRECT FIT

Your focus pads should be a snug fit around your wrist. If they have a Velcro wrist-strap, pull and fasten this before each session: not so tight as to restrict your circulation and chafe your skin, but not so loose that the pads slip up or off your hand, and/or twist around your wrist.

It's not necessary or advisable to wear hand-wraps inside your focus pads: they will simply bunch up and inhibit your grip. Your hands should get enough protection from the padding and air-flow already built into the design, and, if you are holding and using the mitts correctly (see below), your wrists should not require any extra binding or support.

YOUR POSITION/STANCE

As discussed above, during all glove-and-pad work you should copy your client's stance. As well as being (and looking) professional, taking up the traditional boxing stance while holding the pads enables you to absorb shots more effectively. If you try standing square on, with stiff legs, you will feel how much more strongly the impact of your client's punches resounds through your body.

Bear in mind too that 'standing' or static drills, in which you simply hold up the pads for your client to hit, can be beneficial – but this is nothing compared to what you can achieve on the move, as you introduce footwork and defence into the mix. And, as has already been emphasised, you can't move effectively as a boxer or a boxing trainer unless you are in the correct stance.

As well as standing correctly, in a nice, relaxed position ready to receive your client's punches and combinations, make sure you look *at* your client – *all the time*. This may seem glaringly obvious, but you'd be surprised how many trainers screw up their eyes or look away as the shots come towards them. How can you position and move the focus pads correctly if you're not even looking? Keep your eyes open, firmly on your client, and with your own chin tucked down as illustrated.

DON'T KEEP BOTH PADS UP ALL THE TIME

As mentioned on page 66, don't simply hold both pads up in the air all the time and expect your client to know what punch or combination you require. This will confuse them, and really tire out your arms.

Call out the shots, and as you do so, raise the appropriate pad or pads in turn. This has the dual advantage of indicating what you're looking for, as well as encouraging the client to watch carefully and react with good reflexes. The pad you're not using can simply be held at waist level, loosely against your body (as illustrated above right): avoid waving it about in a distracting manner or the client may think you want them to hit it.

Equally, don't point the spare pad directly down at the ground with a straight arm, as it will take too long for you to raise it as and when it is required.

If you are moving around with your client, interspersing footwork with shots and combinations, hold both pads at your waist during the footwork, or up in the guard position as if they were boxing gloves.

You may find it a bit awkward or confusing to work in this way at first, but you will get used to it. This is a much more professional, engaged and effective way in which to use the focus pads.

ANGLING AND POSITIONING THE PADS

Each trainer is different, and develops their own style, flair and idiosyncrasies when using the focus pads – just as each client is an individual, physically and by way of temperament. You will need to get used to holding the pads for all kinds of people: male, female, young, old, tall, short, heavy, light, anxious, confident… If your services are in demand, at some stage you are likely to encounter them all.

Because everyone is different, you also need to be able to 'read' your clients sensitively, responding not only to their current fitness level and technical ability, but also to their fluctuating moods and energy resources. Everyone has their up and down days. It does nobody any good to be pushed beyond what they are capable of in any particular session; by contrast, it may really help someone on a particular day to be chivvied out of their fatigue or low mood. *Talk* to your clients; ask them how they feel; pick up on any unspoken signs of tiredness or illness; and tailor their workout accordingly. This is your job – be great at it.

In terms of how you position and angle the focus pads for specific drills, shots and combinations, there are few hard-and-fast rules. As long as what you do is safe and effective, you can make the pads your own and enjoy putting a unique stamp on your work. However, there are some basic guidelines that you should follow for good technique and injury prevention, and these are set out below.

HOW HIGH SHOULD YOU HOLD THE PADS?

You may need to vary the height at which you hold the focus pads – taking into account how tall your client is relative to you. Ideally, you'll hold the pads as described on page 66: just above your own shoulder height, on either side of your face, and about shoulder-width apart. This enables you to absorb the impact of shots by 'giving' a little at the shoulders, aided by the natural muscular support offered by your upper back. (Your elbows also help with the shock absorption; don't let them stray too far out from your body like chicken wings – especially when receiving hooks, as described below.)

However, if you have a client who is a lot shorter or a lot taller than you, you will need to be flexible regarding the positioning of your pads. If you aren't, the client will end up either having to 'reach' up to you, or having to punch downwards. There may be occasions on which you actually *want* them to do so for a particular training effect, but having to box like this all the time will strain

Figure 15.2(a) Holding the pads correctly – either side of the face, but close in to the body.

Figure 15.2(b) Incorrect – there is too much extension at the elbow joints.

their muscles and interfere with their technique. So be sure to adjust accordingly, while remaining within your own comfort zone.

With shorter clients, you may choose to adjust by bending at the knees to bring yourself down to an appropriate level, rather than moving the pads down your body. With taller clients, holding the pads up much higher than the level of your shoulders can be quite a strain. This is made worse if they are strong, heavy hitters, because you no longer have the support of your upper back to help absorb the impact; the shoulder joint and rotator cuff muscles take all the punishment. In such cases you may need to limit the pad work you do, focusing instead on the punch bag and other boxing fitness elements. Another option is to be a bit crafty, and make them do drills like punching continuously while in a squat, bringing *them* down to *your* level!

FOR STRAIGHT SHOTS AND COMBINATIONS 'TO THE HEAD'

Hold the focus pads with the front of each mitt directly facing your client. It may feel natural to angle the pads inwards slightly, towards each other – but don't overdo this, or you may encourage incorrect technique in your client's shots. You don't want straight punches to start straying into hook territory. As you look ahead, you should see mostly the back of your hands, fitting snugly into the glove part of the mitt.

The pads should always act as a natural extension of your hands. As you are holding them up in the 'ready' position, check to see that the flat face of each pad forms a continuous, vertical line with your forearm

Among inexperienced trainers, a common error is to angle the pads towards the ground by tilting the hands forwards at the wrists. This fault may be accompanied by too much extension at the elbow joints (see figure 15.2b), as the instructor – justifiably a bit nervous as the punches come his or her way – attempts to move the target away from their body/face. By contrast, some instructors hunch up their shoulders and hold the pads tensely, far too close to their body – going so far as to angle the wrists backwards, or even outwards as if doing the a royal wave. Imagine the strain on their joints, and the difficulty experienced by the client in making effective contact with the focus pads.

It's quite easy to avoid these errors if you just relax. Keep your wrists strong (but not rigidly fixed), so that the whole forearm makes a kind of 'unit' with the pad, and hold the pads on either side of your face – not too far apart, which will make your shoulders very vulnerable. It can help to adopt the classic 'Don't shoot!' position from the movies. Figure 15.2 clearly shows the correct angle and position of the focus pads for straight shots and combinations.

FOR STRAIGHT SHOTS AND COMBINATIONS 'TO THE BODY'

For a straight shot to the body, you have a choice as to how to position the receiving focus pad. Some trainers like to keep it in the same position as for a shot to the head, simply lowering their hand from shoulder to torso/waist level (maintaining the strong wrist and forearm) to indicate that the punch is to be thrown further down. Depending on how (legally) low the blow that's required, they may also squat at the knees to bring the pad down to the correct level (see figure 15.3).

This technique is fine for basic jabs and rear hands to the body – although it may fail to offer sufficient support for the trainer's wrists and

Figure 15.3 Holding the pad for a jab 'to the body'.

shoulders if their client is a heavy hitter. However, it will make life difficult for hooks to the body (see below), which may come in at a range of different angles and positions.

The alternative way of holding the pad for a body shot is very difficult to describe in words! Refer to figure 15.5, and you will see how the pad that is to receive the punch is turned inwards, with the palm/mitt still facing out from the instructor's body. (If the receiving pad is in your left hand, the

movement will be clockwise; for the right hand, it will be anti-clockwise.)

To effect the change of hand position, the elbow will necessarily travel in a slight outward arc, away from the body. To receive the shot, the pad can be variously angled and positioned, depending on the punch or combination you have requested of your client. When introducing novices to body shots, you may wish to hold the focus pad away from your body a little … just in case they miss! For the

Figure 15.4 For a hook 'to the head'.

sake of comfort and/or extra support, you have the option of placing the non-receiving pad on top of the receiving one, as shown in figure 15.5.

FOR HOOKS 'TO THE HEAD'

This is quite a simple change of pad position for the trainer. Instead of the front face of the mitt facing outwards, towards the client, you simply turn the receiving hand inwards by around 90 degrees – towards the mid-line of your body as shown in figure 15.4. (If you were to do the same with both pads simultaneously, they would be facing each other.) The non-receiving hand needs to drop down so as not to impede the incoming shot.

When receiving a hook, be careful just to move your hand, and not the whole of your forearm – or even your whole arm. A common error among novice boxing instructors is to open out the angle at their elbow, by moving the receiving pad laterally away from the face. This not only makes it difficult for the client to achieve the correct technique and contact for the hook, it also weakens your arm by taking away the 'giving' support of the shoulder and upper back. With a hard hitter, or simply by way of attrition over time, you could well injure your rotator cuff or otherwise strain your shoulder joint.

FOR HOOKS 'TO THE BODY'

To receive hooks to the body at various levels and angles, you will need to hold the pad as shown in figure 15.5, and as described on pages 53-4. The most common place to position the receiving pad is at the instructor's hip, but obviously you have to be able to vary this to ensure accurate pad

Figure 15.5 For a hook 'to the body'.

placement – and thus protect your own torso! – in response to your client's incoming shots.

This technique is advanced and can be quite tricky to master, but does get easier with practice. The best advice is not to progress to this type of body shot until you are confident that your client's hooks won't be too wild, and that your pad work is at the appropriate stage in your own training development.

FOR UPPERCUTS

Receiving uppercuts requires a simple tilt of the relevant focus pad, so that the contact surface is facing down – ready for your client's vertical shot as if the pad were an imaginary opponent's chin.

You will need to develop some measure of skill in assessing how high to hold the focus pad for the uppercut, according to how tall the client is relative to yourself. Don't hold the mitt too low: this is a common fault. Think realistically about where the punch would land if this were a boxing bout, and adjust accordingly. You may also choose to place your non-active hand on top of the receiving focus pad, to provide additional support and stability, especially if your client is a hard-hitter (see figure 15.7).

When you tilt the pad, make sure that you don't just bend your hand at the wrist. This will afford your joints no strength or protection, and the shot is likely to flick or bend your hand back painfully. Instead, keep a strong wrist and achieve the change in pad position by moving your whole forearm. Depending on how high you are having to lift the pad, your elbow is likely to part company with your torso a little; that's OK, but try always to keep it below the horizontal and your hand slightly higher than the elbow, as shown in figure 15.6.

Figure 15.6 Holding the pad for a (southpaw) lead hand uppercut.

Figure 15.7 For additional support and stability, place the non-receiving pad on top.

ACTIVE VERSUS PASSIVE – HOW MUCH SHOULD YOU MOVE THE PADS TOWARDS THE CLIENT?

This is a very good question and the subject of some debate. Some technicians advocate holding the pads completely still (obviously, once they have been raised into the correct position to receive the punch or combination). The main argument in favour of this is that it encourages the client to punch at full extension, through the pad, much as a sprinter will run through the finish line rather than stopping dead when they get there.

> We teach our coaches *not* to 'feed' the focus pads back to the boxer – not to move them out towards his or her gloves as s/he punches. If they do so, the boxer will think the punch or combination is finished too early, as soon as they make contact. They will then retract their hand(s) too soon and, in a contest, risk falling short with their shots. (GB Regional Coach, Amateur Boxing Association)

However, other instructors believe it's better to make a slight movement towards the client with the pads, for several reasons:

> In my opinion, moving the focus pads towards the client assists them by giving them a subtle reminder of the punches or combinations you're asking for. This is especially helpful when they're just starting out. It also serves to absorb the impact of the punches and so is much easier on my shoulders. (Personal trainer, South East London)

> I find 'feeding' the pads to the client works much better in terms of motivation. In boxing fitness, plenty of people don't punch that hard but they still like to feel powerful. If you move the pads towards them, their shots will make a nice 'thwack' instead of being soaked up like a sponge. As the client get stronger and improves technically, you can gradually reduce the amount of active engagement on your part while still achieving an audible result. But *always be careful not to overdo it*: you should *never* slap out hard or aggressively with the focus pads, as this can be scary for the client and risks damaging their hands or wrists – as well as tiring you out excessively. (Clinton McKenzie, British and European champion and boxing fitness pioneer)

Feel your way: over time and with practice, you will find the ideal balance.

BASIC DRILLS ON THE FOCUS PADS

16

The particular focus pad drills you choose to practise with your client will obviously depend on how fit they are, and how proficient in the boxing techniques. You won't ask a novice for complicated combinations of hooks and uppercuts, any more than you will restrict an experienced boxer to straight shots. Having said that, when structuring your focus pad sessions, there are other things to consider:

- You need to be realistic about your own facility with the pads. Don't work outside your comfort zone, asking clients for skills that you yourself aren't up to teaching or delivering. Remember, this is boxing fitness; there is no need for you to be a technical expert. As long as you are challenging, motivating and taking each client forward according to their individual fitness goals, you are doing your job.
- Only good can come of practising the basics. We have already spoken about the importance of muscle memory in boxing – indeed, in any sport or fitness activity – and going over the fundamental teaching points for correct punches and combinations, defence and footwork will always be beneficial to your clients. Don't be scared to get them to repeat simple

drills. Not only will it make them better at the boxing techniques, it will get them fitter at the same time.
- Bear in mind the range of ways in which you can work your clients harder to promote fitness gains. Although there is much to be said for variety in terms of drills and techniques – keeping them motivated and challenged, mentally as well as physically – you can also vary the *intensity* of their sessions at any time, by (a) increasing duration, and/or (b) increasing speed, and/or (c) increasing power.

STATIC DRILLS

These consist of punches and combinations repeated a set number of times, with both you and your client remaining stationary: i.e. using no footwork. Static drills are useful as a focus pad warm-up, but make sure you do them after, not instead of, the general warm-up (see pages 23–4). To avoid injury and reduce post-workout stiffness, joints and muscles should always be properly prepared for exercise before beginning any boxing techniques.

After checking your client's stance and guard, and quickly running through the key teaching points for each of the shots and combinations you have selected, perform them, say, ten times each. You might choose five drills, or ten, for each session. Don't repeat exactly the same selection, in the same order, every time. Not only will that quickly get boring, but it will also limit the range of muscles and muscle groups worked.

For ease of reference, you may refer to a particular punch or combination as one repetition (rep); your chosen number of reps (here, ten) comprises a set. Between sets, allow the client sufficient time to catch their breath if necessary, and to consider the next technique you are requesting.

Any or all of the following are good stationary drills for your client to practise on the pads. Start simple and progress to the more complicated. If you have ideas of your own, that's great, but be sure to practise the necessary movements with the focus pads first, before you introduce the drills to your client.

- 10 x jab
- 10 x cross/back hand
- 10 x double jab
- 10 x double jab-cross/back hand
- 10 x one-two
- 10 x one-two-double jab (encourage a slight pause before the double jab)
- 10 x double jab-one-two (encourage a slight pause before the one-two)
- 10 x three straight
- 10 x four straight
- 10 x one-two-lead hand hook
- 10 x one-two-lead hand hook-cross/back hand
- 10 x one-two-lead hand uppercut
- 10 x one-two-lead hand uppercut-cross/back hand
- 10 x three straight-rear hand uppercut

- 10 x jab to the head-jab to the body
- 10 x jab to the head-jab to the body-cross/back hand to the head
- 10 x jab to the head-cross/back hand to the body-lead hand hook-cross/back hand to the head

As you and your clients become more proficient at the drills, do the same ones – faster. Increasing punching speed is one of the best ways in which to hike up someone's heart rate, but make sure that in doing so, you don't start slapping out with the pads. It is your client who is doing the hard physical work, not you. Your job is to encourage, motivate, comment constructively and praise. The same caveat applies if you choose to ask for more power. When you consider your client to be fit enough, you could try all the same drills but allow little or no recovery between sets.

INTRODUCE FOOTWORK AND/OR DEFENCE

The next step might be to introduce some simple footwork (see pages 36–41) and/or some defences (see pages 68–74) into the mix. Again, whatever you choose to ask of your client, remind them about the key technical points first. There is a lot for them to learn and remember, which is both the challenge and the beauty of boxing fitness in general, and of focus pad work in particular.

For your chosen shot or combination, you could perform each rep followed by a forward, backward or sideways step – or a combination of these. So, for example, you might ask for:

- 5 x double jab-cross/back hand-step forwards; 5 x double jab-cross/back hand-step back, followed by

- 5 x one-two-hook-step to the right; 5 x one-two-hook-step to the left

Or, to incorporate defence, you could try:

- 10 x four straight-push-away-step back in, *followed by*
- 10 x four straight-duck

Or, you could be even more ambitious and use both footwork and defence, for example:

- 10 x one-two-roll inside the jab-step to the side-counter with a hook-cross/back hand!

As your skills, confidence and training relationship with each client develop, you will discover more and more ways in which you can build, vary and fine-tune your repertoire of drills.

BUILD DURATION – SINGLE AND MULTIPLE ROUNDS

With the introduction and practice of single shots + combinations + footwork + defence, you have the foundation for a full round of active, effective focus pad work. And with the achievement of a full round, you have the option of adding any number of further rounds, depending on your client's current fitness level and their short- and longer-term goals. This is great for you, because it enables flexible, open-ended training and progressive physiological adaptation.

To be realistic in replicating the fitness demands of actual boxing, a full round of focus pads should be of two or three minutes' duration. There must always be a whole minute of recovery allowed between each round, no matter how long the round itself; however, remember that you can make things harder or easier for each client as required, by giving them more or less rest between actual work efforts. Sensing how to space these work efforts appropriately, piling on or easing up on the pressure, is part of the focus pad instructor's skill, and one which you will develop over time.

During the round(s), while your clients are getting their breath back between shots and combinations, remind them to inhale deeply ('Come on – suck it up!') and to stay in their stance with their guard up. It may be tempting for them, when pushed, to drop their hands, lean on the ropes of the boxing ring or even crouch down. Boxers wouldn't do any of these, so neither should they. They will recover better if they remain upright, breathing properly and focusing on the next technique you'll be requesting, in order to take their mind off the pain.

Don't expect any client to be able to go from a few static focus pad drills to a full three-minute round without due progression. This will be too much, both physically and psychologically. Instead, use your professional judgement and experience to phase your combined efforts as appropriate to their level of general fitness, boxing skills, and confidence in their own abilities. Build things up gradually until you're able to congratulate them (and yourself) on achieving a great focus pad workout. Keeping – or encouraging them to keep – a training diary to record their improvements, and to put any 'off' days into perspective, can really help with their motivation… and therefore with your client retention.

THINKING 'OUTSIDE THE BOXING'

17

This chapter is concerned with some lateral thinking. Every good exercise professional needs to be creative if they are to keep the sessions and programmes they design both fresh and challenging. In the introduction to this *Complete Guide*, the point was made that boxing fitness training is fabulously flexible – not just because the instructor is able to tailor-make a client's workouts to his or her individual requirements; nor because the sessions can be done at any venue, any time. The important consideration here is that you don't have to stay with the traditional boxing techniques. As

long as what you do is safe and underpinned by sound exercise principles, you can experiment to your heart's content.

In the pages directly following, you'll find some suggestions for tried-and-tested focus pad drills and exercises that incorporate boxing-related techniques, but which you are unlikely to see put into practice in a competitive boxing ring. The sport's purists may frown on such unconventional elements, but you are free to introduce them into your clients' sessions, because 'safety' – in terms of their defence against an opponent – is not your prime consideration. This is boxing fitness. There is no glove-to-body contact, so your client will never get hit. You may well have introduced defensive manoeuvres into their training repertoire, but you've done so for the sake of variety and to achieve particular physiological adaptations, not because you need to teach them to protect themselves against another boxer.

So, let loose! Try out some or all of the drills described below, and then think up your own. Get together with some colleagues and brainstorm; share what you're doing, and combine ideas to come up with brand new trials and tribulations for your poor, unsuspecting guinea-pig clients or pupils.

DRILLS INCORPORATING SQUATS – CORE STABILITY AND LOWER-BODY STRENGTH/TONING
FOCUS PAD PYRAMID

Holding the pads, face your client, both of you standing square on (see page 34). You can also do this drill in the boxing stance, but you'll need to be sure regularly to swap from southpaw to orthodox to maintain a balanced workout for both lead legs. Get your client to throw a four straight combination followed directly by a squat (or duck – see pages 68–9). This comprises one rep. You can squat with them if you like. Ensure that all squats are performed with good technique, i.e. with feet and knees pointing forwards and the spine neutral. Perform the rep ten times before moving down the pyramid as described below. At the bottom of the pyramid, allow the client a brief recovery before working their way back up.

You can repeat this drill as many times as you like. It's excellent both for cardiorespiratory fitness and for lower-body strength and toning, as it uses all the large muscle groups in the legs and buttocks. The straight-shot combinations also work the core.

- Four straight-squat x 10, *followed by*
- Three straight-squat x 10, *followed by*
- One-two-squat x 10, *followed by*
- 5 x jab-squat, 5 x cross/back hand-squat, *followed by*
- *30 seconds' recovery*
- 5 x jab-squat, 5 x cross/back hand-squat, *followed by*
- One-two-squat x 10, *followed by*
- Three straight-squat x 10, *followed by*
- Four straight-squat x 10

ISOMETRIC SQUATS

You and your client both perform a squat, holding the position at the bottom of the movement to create an isometric muscle contraction. Perform ten straight shots on the focus pads, before straightening up. Repeat the rep ten times, over any number of sets, with 30 seconds' recovery between sets.

This drill burns – in a good way, and you can make it still more effective by slowing the squatting movement right down (both on the descent and on the way back up). It is excellent toning and strength work for the lower body, as well as aiding core stability.

Vary the drill by, say, substituting squats for slow calf raises, or changing the emphasis of the squat by turning the feet out so that the inner

Figure 17.1 Focus pad pyramid – squat then punch.

Figure 17.2 Isometric squats – punch while in the squat.

thigh muscles are especially targeted. Or get the client to try squatting on one leg …

DRILLS SPECIFICALLY FOR CORE STRENGTH/STABILITY
SINGLE-PAD WORK

Face your client, both of you in the boxing stance. Hold up a single focus pad – left or right – and instruct your client to perform a ten-punch, straight-shot combination on it. This will feel weird to them, because they are accustomed to hitting alternate pads in the usual way. Make sure they persevere.

Then hold up the other pad, and ask for the same combination. Repeat the drill twice more so that they are effectively switching from right to left focus pads to perform each 'ten straight'. Three lots of ten on each pad is one set.

This is a very tiring drill, and you may find that two or three sets, with 30 seconds' rest between each, is sufficient to induce both cardiorespiratory

Figure 17.3 Single-pad work.

and muscle fatigue. Its efficacy stems from the client having to box 'across' their body, directing the shots at a smaller target and working to a much narrower focus than they are used to.

'THE Y DRILL'

Face your client, both of you standing 'square on' rather than in the boxing stance (see page 34). Hold the focus pads out to your sides, quite far apart so that your body forms a kind of Y-shape as shown in figure 17.4. Angle the pads inwards slightly, as though you are about to receive alternate hooks. Keep your wrists, elbows and shoulders strong in preparation for your client's shots.

The client twists at the midriff and punches each pad in turn. Instead of keeping a fixed angle at their elbows as per the hook technique, they purposely extend the arm at the elbow as they punch. The hips remain facing forwards; all of the body movement comes from the waist.

For this drill, choose whatever number of reps you like: 10, 20, 30 punches, repeated over however many sets, with a brief rest in between each set. Encourage the client to build up rhythm and momentum for quite powerful contact with the pads.

Try the same drill, but on the move. Shuffle backwards as you hold the pads, so the client has to advance. Then change direction so you are advancing and they are moving backwards. Or, try incorporating some squats.

Note: To avoid any strain or injury to the lower back, always perform this drill towards the end of a workout, ensuring that the client is well warmed up. Avoid it altogether in those with back problems; and avoid it, too, if your shoulders are or become sore, or if your client is particularly tall or strong.

Figure 17.4 The Y drill – excellent core training.

'AXES AND PLANES'

This drill switches continuously between straight shots, uppercuts, and hooks, in order to achieve movement around all the axes and planes of the body – fantastic for the core. Perform as follows, for one repetition:

- Stand facing your client, both of you in the boxing stance.
- Hold the pads for a four straight, *then*

Figure 17.5 Axes and planes: straight shots (a) followed by uppercuts (b) followed by hooks (c).

- Reposition the pads for four uppercuts, alternating (left-right-left-right, or right-left-right-left according to the stance), *then*
- Reposition the pads for four hooks, alternating (as above).

Repeat this sequence five times to make one set. Do five sets, giving the client a short rest between each.

You could think up lots of variations. For example, instead of setting a particular number of punches (here the sequence is [4 + 4 + 4 x 5] x 5), perform the shots over a specified time period. Try 30 seconds of continuous straight shots, followed by 30 seconds of alternating uppercuts, followed by 30 seconds of alternating hooks. This 90-second effort comprises one set. Repeat three or five times, giving the client a minute's rest between each set. Ultimately you can build up to a minute of each type of shot, so that the client is actually performing a full round of continuous punching.

DRILLS FOR THE ABDOMINALS

The client lies on their back with their feet flat on the floor and knees bent. They are wearing their boxing gloves. You kneel or sit lightly on or at their feet, holding the focus pads. They sit up, throw four straight punches, then lie back down again: this is one rep. Repeat ten times for a set, and repeat the sets any number of times with an appropriate recovery between each.

For variety, try holding the pads further up above their body, so they have to reach higher, or closer to your shoulders so they have to reach out more.

Try getting them to throw four alternating hooks instead of four straight punches, to achieve more of a turn at the waist when they have sat up.

Figure 17.6 Abdominal drills.

Experiment with moving the pads closer together and further apart.

Or get them to punch out with both hands simultaneously. Or turn the drill into a pyramid (see page 105), so that for each sit-up they are performing increasing or decreasing numbers of punches.

CARDIO DRILLS

These are perhaps the easiest to think up, because you can incorporate any kind of circuit-type training or sprint work into your focus pad drills in order to kick up your client's heart rate. Here are a few ideas:

- *Lapping*: whatever drill or combination you are working on, get the client to run rings around you – literally – between reps or sets. Alternate direction so they don't get dangerously dizzy.
- *Press-ups* (or sit-ups, or squat thrusts, or star jumps): get them to perform a number of these between each rep or set.
- *Shuttle runs*: especially good in a group environment. Set things up so that you receive, say, ten shots on the pads from each pupil, who then runs back and forth over a set distance, any number of times you choose to dictate. Make it fun; make it into a race.
- *Fast, continuous punching*: change it up, don't limit the client. Try holding the pads up over your head so they have to really reach up to hit them.

PART **FOUR**

DIET AND HEALTH

This section of the book is concerned with matters of diet and health, because these are as essential to your clients' fitness, safety and wellbeing as a correct training protocol and technique. As an exercise professional you already know this; what you may not be quite as aware of – or as good at remembering – is that the same things are essential for you personally.

By working in the fitness industry, you have chosen a job that is physically challenging and sometimes emotionally demanding. Having read the first three parts of this *Complete Guide* you will have realised that this is especially true of boxing fitness, the teaching of which involves far more than holding a stopwatch or counting reps and sets. As an effective boxing trainer, you have to engage both mentally and physically in your clients' workouts.

You may keep long and strange hours, working early in the morning and late into the evening, possibly in inhospitable surroundings such as cold, windy, rainy parks. Between sessions, showers and hand-wrap laundry you have to keep up to date with industry developments, client paperwork,

marketing your services, and your own Continuing Professional Development – in addition to the many other mundane tasks we all have to fit into our days. You probably have little time or energy to lavish on yourself.

Unless you look after yourself, as well as your clients, this kind of lifestyle will take its toll. The success of your livelihood depends directly on the efficient functioning of your body, so that if you neglect its needs, you are risking more than your health; your income and reputation as a reliable, robust fitness professional could also suffer.

And it's not just about the body: there are less tangible things to take into account, which nonetheless confer quality of life – such as rest and recovery, time spent with loved ones, and the enjoyment of hobbies and other leisure pursuits. While you are advising your clients about sound nutritional practices; the importance of good hydration; the prevention and management of minor ailments and injuries; and how to achieve a balance between the conservation and expenditure of their energy resources, you must apply all the same considerations to yourself.

NUTRITION // AND HYDRATION

18

ASSESS THE CLIENT'S DIETARY KNOWLEDGE/ UNDERSTANDING
IMPORTANCE OF THE FOOD DIARY

These days, many people are reasonably well informed about the importance of a balanced diet, and understand that this includes not only appropriate food intake, but also enough of the right kind of fluids. Your clients may already know that a good diet is necessary, not only to keep healthy, but also significantly to increase the likelihood of achieving their fitness objectives. Rather than re-inventing the wheel, have a chat to them about their diet as part of the initial client consultation process (see pages 20–1). In this way you can assess their general level of knowledge and understanding, and narrow down any areas you may need to address.

Ask them to keep a food diary for a few days; a template is provided on page 174. They should write down *everything* they eat and drink, from when they wake up to when they go to bed (and even during the night), together with the approximate time at which they did so. Emphasise that it's important for them to be honest. The food diary is not a 'test' designed to catch them out or make them feel bad about themselves – quite the

opposite; it may reveal the need for some quite simple changes that will make a huge difference to their body composition, energy levels and workout performance.

Explain that the food diary has other benefits, too. It's quite easy to eat or drink without really being aware of the amount and/or the quality of what we are taking in. Alternatively we may do the opposite, neglecting nutrition and hydration in the whirlwind of our busy lifestyles. Keeping an honest food diary provides black-and-white proof of a client's nutritional intake, and will also make them more aware of what they are doing – perhaps staying their hand as they reach for the comfort snacks or pint of beer that they don't really want or need.

When you analyse a client's food diary and make any recommendations for change, you will bring to bear your existing knowledge of sound dietary principles and practice. The basics of good nutrition are summarised briefly below, by way of a useful reminder; you could even reproduce these as a handout for your client to refer to as necessary.

As well as thinking generally, bear in mind any specific demands placed on your clients' bodies by the boxing fitness workout. During boxing sessions, you and your client will sweat profusely:

adequate hydration and rehydration are essential. And because the sessions comprise mainly high-intensity, interval-type training, it is paramount that their diet includes sufficient of the right type of carbohydrate.

SOUND DIETARY PRINCIPLES AND PRACTICE – A SUMMARY

Your client will need to understand the following:

- That the human body requires food in order to rebuild or repair itself, and to provide fuel (energy) for its systems to function.

- That this food comprises three main groups of nutrient: carbohydrate, protein and fat.
- That their body also requires an intake of vitamins and minerals in order to help release the energy contained within food; and sufficient of the right kind of fluids to keep their bodies well hydrated.

CARBOHYDRATE – FUNCTIONS AND TYPES/SOURCES

Carbohydrate fuels muscle contractions, and so is the main energy source for any exercise, including boxing fitness. At low training intensities, fat (see

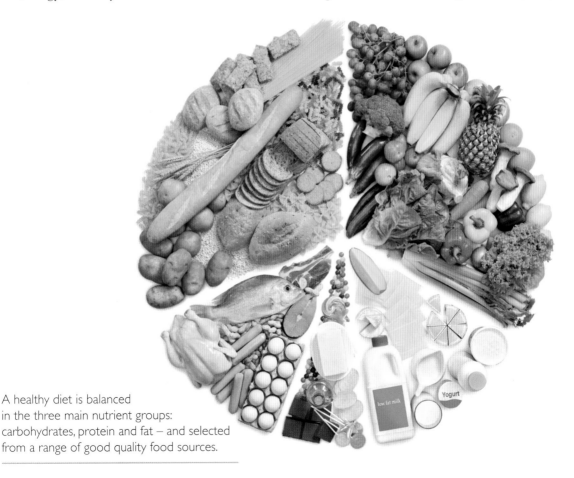

A healthy diet is balanced
in the three main nutrient groups:
carbohydrates, protein and fat – and selected
from a range of good quality food sources.

below) is the body's preferred source of fuel – as long as no carbohydrate is readily available; but as training intensity increases, carbohydrate becomes the preferred source. Recommended carb intake is around 5–7g per kilo of bodyweight per day for an individual in hard training, or 210–490g for a 70kg athlete.

Once eaten, carbohydrate is digested and used in the body in a number of ways:

- It is broken down into glucose and carried in the bloodstream before being used by the tissues as fuel. The passage of glucose from the blood into the body's tissues is controlled by the hormone insulin, which plays a vital role in regulating blood sugar levels. If the body does not produce sufficient insulin, or its cells are unable to respond to the insulin that is produced, the disease known as diabetes results.

- Any carbohydrate that is not needed for immediate energy release is stored in the muscles and liver, as glycogen.

- Once the body's carbohydrate stores are full, any excess present in the blood is converted to fat.

If the body doesn't have enough carbohydrate to meet its energy demands, protein will be broken down: this can limit the ability to build and maintain tissues. Carbs are also an energy source for the brain and central nervous system, playing a vital role in activities that require thought, precision, dexterity and coordination – activities such as boxing training.

Carbs may be simple (also referred to as 'sugars') or complex (including those known as 'starches'). A third type of carbohydrate is known as 'fibre'. Simple carbs are easy to digest, and are thus readily made available to the body as fuel. Fruit is a good source, being cheap and convenient, as well as containing the micronutrients necessary to release the food's energy potential. Unfortunately, other, very tasty, sources of simple carbohydrate include biscuits, cakes, confectionery and soft drinks such as cola; these contain excessive sugar and may also contain fat, and should be limited in the diet or, ideally, avoided altogether.

Complex carbs take longer to be broken down, absorbed into the bloodstream and stored or used by the body. This means that the fuel they contain is released more slowly over a sustained period, giving a steady, constant energy supply.

The nutritional value of complex carbs further depends on whether they are refined or unrefined. Refined carbohydrates (e.g. white bread, pasta and rice) are generally processed, and thus often lower in fibre, vitamins and minerals. Unrefined carbohydrates (e.g. wholemeal or wholegrain products; fresh and frozen vegetables) have not been processed to the same extent, and are therefore healthier choices.

Fibre is basically indigestible plant material: it is found in fruits, vegetables, grains and beans. Fibre doesn't provide the body with any energy,

but may help lower blood cholesterol. It can also slow the delivery of glucose into the bloodstream, which in turn may reduce the risk of developing some forms of diabetes and coronary heart disease; they also make an individual feel fuller/less hungry for longer.

In summary, your client needs to understand that carbohydrate is the main fuel for their boxing fitness sessions, and to make sure they have sufficient stores available in their muscles to go the distance. How long their energy supply will last depends on the duration and intensity of the workout you have set them. As a general rule, if the session is much longer than an hour, or if the client hasn't eaten within two hours prior to exercising, you will advise them to replenish their glycogen stores with a carb-rich snack or sports drink (see page 122).

Check that their diet includes plenty of complex, unrefined carbohydrates – to keep their energy stores topped-up, and to provide a steady, sustained release of energy. Good choices are wholegrain pasta and rice, sweet potato, porridge and breakfast cereals. Explain that simple/unrefined carbs can give them an energy boost, but the 'spikes' in blood sugar that they cause may leave them feeling low and tired at certain times of the day.

PROTEIN – FUNCTIONS AND TYPES/SOURCES

Protein has the following functions:

- It forms the framework of many bodily structures, including collagen (present in bone and connective tissue); keratin (present in the skin); and muscle tissue.
- Especially during endurance events or periods of fasting, protein provides a useable source of energy.
- It also regulates various bodily processes, such as controlling blood sugar levels and fighting infection.

All proteins are made from amino acids, and there are 20 amino acids in total. Of these, nine are generally considered to be essential to the daily diet, because the body cannot produce them independently; we have to ingest them in our food. However, the specific amino acids considered to be essential may change at different stages of life, while this definition may vary slightly among different experts.

Proteins containing all of the essential amino acids are known as 'complete'. Most sources of complete proteins are animal-based (eggs, meat, poultry, dairy and fish). Plants such as grains, cereals, nuts, seeds and vegetables do contain protein, but they are 'incomplete' sources, being deficient in one or more of the essential amino acids. So it is especially important, if your client is a vegetarian, to make sure they include a variety of protein sources in their diet – thus making up the full complement of amino acids over the course of a day.

The human body breaks down proteins continuously, recycling their component amino acids to build new proteins elsewhere. This process can be intensified during exercise, with the secretion of a hormone called cortisol. Cortisol acts to maintain the body's energy supply, by variously breaking down carbohydrate, protein and fats.

While the body's preferred source of energy is carbohydrate, when all the available carbs have been used up the body will turn to protein as a source of fuel. So, depending on your client's diet, and on the duration and intensity of their boxing fitness sessions, some muscle tissue breakdown may occur as a result of their exercise programme. It's therefore important to make sure they are including some protein in all of their meals, and that they are resting and eating well after each training session – thus helping to encourage and promote tissue growth and repair.

Protein should make up at least 10% of your client's overall diet, or a minimum of 0.8g per kilo of bodyweight (around 55g per day for a 70kg athlete). Eating excessive amounts will just result in the excess being excreted in urine or used as fuel. However, if the client is losing weight, their body is more likely to burn protein as a fuel, particularly as available carbohydrate is often reduced during calorie restriction.

Similarly, those looking to gain lean mass will have higher protein requirements, and regularly participating in exercise increases protein requirements above those of inactive people. The

International Society for Sports Nutrition identifies those undertaking weight-loss regimes as those with the highest protein requirements per kilo! During weight loss or weight gain, requirements may increase to 1.4–1.7g per kilo of bodyweight per day, or 100–120g per day for a 70kg athlete.

For this and other reasons, advise your clients to eat protein as part of small, regular meals. Recommended daily allowances (RDAs) vary for each individual, and depend on many factors: more information is available from your national Food Standards Agency.

When advising your clients on protein intake, consider that the boxing fitness workout is energetic and endurance based, and may bring about muscle tissue breakdown. Make sure they are including some protein in all of their meals –

good sources to recommend are fresh, quality meat, eggs, raw nuts, milk, and tinned beans or pulses in water. All whey protein products are by-products of dairy, and contain exceptionally high-quality proteins.

Clients should vary between semi-skimmed and whole milk, depending on their weight requirements. Younger clients aged under 18 haven't yet fully developed their glycogen-burning capacity, and so would be well advised to consume full fat dairy for fuelling exercise and growth.

Remind clients that the body can only utilise a certain amount of protein at any one time, so it's better to eat little and often; and that processing and overheating their food will denature the protein in it.

FAT – FUNCTIONS AND TYPES/ SOURCES

Fats and oils – together known as lipids – have many important functions in the body, including:

- The formation of cell membranes.
- Assisting in the transmission of nerve impulses.
- Protecting the internal organs (although if there is too much fat present, this can inhibit their function).
- Transporting, storing and utilising some key vitamins.
- Insulating the body, thus helping to regulate body heat.
- Providing an energy reserve for the body.

Dietary fat is often vilified, being linked in the public consciousness with obesity, heart disease and other disabling conditions. But just like carbohydrate and protein, fat is an essential nutrient and should comprise around 30% of a person's overall food intake. Emphasise to the client that fat itself is not the problem – it is the type, source and amount that matter.

Fat has more than twice the calories per gram of both carbohydrate and protein, so diets high in any kind of fat are *energy dense* – in other words, they may lead to us taking in more energy than we use up, thereby promoting an increase in body fat. It is excessive body fat, not dietary fat itself, that is a danger to our health and has been linked to the development of disease.

- *Saturated fats*, which are solid at room temperature, are found naturally in meat, poultry, dairy and eggs, as well as in non-animal sources such as palm and coconut oils. Although studies have linked saturated fats with 'clogged arteries', in fact they are an essential part of our diet, enhancing the immune system and helping to promote healthy liver function.

- *Unsaturated oils*, which are liquid at room temperature, fall under two main categories:

'monounsaturated' and 'polyunsaturated'. Sources of the first include olive oil, avocados, nuts and seeds; while the latter are found in oily fish, sunflower seeds and oil, walnuts, pumpkin seeds and sesame seeds.

Both types of unsaturated fat are necessary for health. Diets high in monounsaturated fats are thought to lower blood cholesterol levels, thus reducing the risk of coronary heart disease. Polyunsaturates are sources of omega 3 and 6 – substances that cannot be synthesised by the body, but are important for healthy cell functioning.

Trans fats, also referred to as *hydrogenated fats*, should be avoided in the diet where possible. Some do occur naturally, but the majority are a by-product of manufacturing, and are therefore present in heavily processed foods such as biscuits, cakes, pies and pastries. Trans fats have no positive use in the body, but are simply stored as body fat – simultaneously preventing other, 'good' types of fat from fulfilling their required functions.

Stress to your clients that even if losing weight (reducing their body fat – see below) is one of their fitness goals, they should not cut out fat from their diet. Instead, they should limit and balance their overall fat intake. Advise them to avoid skimmed or artificially low-fat foods: these have been processed and often 'padded out' with trans fats. Instead, they should choose quality meats, dairy, seeds and oily fish, as well as butter, olive and coconut oil.

A HEALTHY DIET – IN SUMMARY

It is clear from the above that we all need to consume a diet that is balanced in the three main nutrient groups, roughly in the following proportions:

- Carbohydrate: around 5–7g per kilo of body-weight per day for an individual in hard training; or 210–490g for a 70kg athlete.
- Protein: 10–20% – a minimum of 0.8g per kilo of bodyweight (around 55g per day for a 70kg

athlete). During weight loss or weight gain, requirements may increase to 1.4–1.7g per kilo of bodyweight per day, or 100–120g per day for a 70kg athlete.

- Fat: aim for a starting point of 30%; vary this amount according to weight loss/weight gain goals.

Remind clients that it is not just the balance of nutrients that is important: we should all be careful to select from varied, good-quality food sources. Many factors along the food chain – from soil to seed to animal welfare; from the use of chemicals for growth and ripening, to methods of transportation, manufacturing and processing – affect the quality of the food that leaves the farm and eventually arrives on our plates. It is important to make sensible, informed dietary choices that suit our lifestyle and preferences, while still ensuring long-term health and wellbeing.

DIET, EXERCISE AND WEIGHT LOSS/GAIN

In all likelihood, the majority of your boxing fitness clients will be exercising not just for their health, but also because they wish to 'lose weight'. You will know that this terminology is in fact misleading, because what a person weighs on the bathroom scales – their body mass – is a combination of both fat and lean tissue, which includes bone, muscles, ligaments and tendons.

Body composition as one of the key elements of fitness may be defined as 'the amount of body fat a person carries relative to their lean tissue mass, expressed as a percentage'. If your client asks you for a guide, it is generally considered healthy for a man to have a body fat percentage of 10–20%, and a woman 15–25%. But these figures are influenced by many factors, including personal preferences, culture and tradition, and an elite athlete's ideal body composition will vary significantly from these figures according to the particular requirements of their sport.

MEASURING AND ANALYSING BODY COMPOSITION

For most fitness professionals, working out a client's body fat percentage is actually quite tricky to do. Common and widely accessible methods of measuring body fat include the body mass index, or BMI, which bases its calculations on an individual's height and weight; and bioelectrical impedance analysis, or BIA, as found in many of today's digital scales. This sends a low-level, safe, electrical current through the body to arrive at a calculation of fat mass and fat-free mass. But each of these methods has its limitations, and results may fail to take account of such things as a person's natural body type and build.

During your training you will have learned a variety of ways in which to measure body composition reasonably accurately. One such is the use of skinfold calipers (a useful recap of this method is at www.acefitness.org/calculators/body fat-calculator. aspx). However, many people really dislike having their measurements taken in this way, because it can be uncomfortable both physically and psychologically. Other solutions, such as underwater weighing (the immersion method), may get results but are hardly practical, requiring specialist equipment and facilities to which you are unlikely to have access outside an elite sports science unit.

So you will need to take a view on each of your clients, assessing how important body composition is to them – in terms of health, self-image and/or sporting performance – and then match your services to their requirements.

For example, if you are asked to teach an elite marathon runner how to box, you may be fully up to the task in terms of technical coaching, but lack the wherewithal to provide them with current, sport-specific nutritional advice and body composition analysis. If that is the case, you may suggest that they employ an additional professional with whom you can liaise, working as a team to provide a holistic service. Help them to seek out a suitable dietician or sports nutritionist: a good option is to research such an individual with the International Olympic Committee diploma, now the standard in sports nutrition.

However, if your client simply wishes to lose fat mass or gain fat-free mass, this should be within the remit of most well-qualified personal trainers and sports coaches. To analyse, record and keep track of their body composition, you can discuss available options, together with their individual preferences, and act accordingly. In the majority of cases, a reliable pair of weighing scales, used regularly on the same day of the week at the same time of day, combined perhaps with body circumference measurements, will be sufficient for both of your needs.

Above all, encourage your clients to arrive at a realistic appraisal of how they would like to look and feel. They may well find that as the boxing training tones their muscles, boosts their energy levels and gives them more self-confidence, concerns about their weight are alleviated – or disappear altogether.

HYDRATION

Water is lost from the body in urine production, as well as in the processes of breathing and sweating. But a range of other factors, such as environmental temperature, and exercise of course, influence individual hydration needs. Boxing fitness is hard, high-intensity work, and your client is likely to sweat more during their sessions than perhaps they are accustomed to. Point this out, and don't forget yourself in this respect. Both you and your clients should take care to be, and to remain, adequately hydrated.

There are many different opinions as to how much water people should drink, and you will have your own guidelines. Most favour around eight average-sized glasses per day. In the UK, the Food Standards Agency recommends an intake of 1.2 litres daily, but other sources go as far as advocating 2–3 litres; the American Institute of Medicine stipulates that men should drink about 13 cups of fluid daily, and women should drink nine. The truth is that it's almost impossible to generalise – and over-consumption can be as bad as

A note on 'sports drinks'

On pages 113–16 we have already discussed carbohydrate as the body's primary energy source, essential for intense exercise. Carbohydrate is stored in the muscles in a readily used form called glycogen.

For their boxing fitness programme, your clients will need to ensure an adequate supply of carbs to meet their training needs, and to replenish their levels afterwards. There is some evidence that drinks containing 'high glycaemic index' (readily digested) sugary carbohydrates can help aid sporting performance and recovery; also, that they may aid performance by stimulating parts of the brain involved with motivation – enhancing high-intensity exercise output in the short term.

However, although such drinks may optimise glycogen use and resynthesis, most of your clients will not be exercising long enough or hard enough to necessitate the ingestion of large volumes of sugary drinks. A healthy diet, as discussed in these pages, will be sufficient to meet their energy needs.

Particularly for younger athletes, the habitual use of sports drinks should not be encouraged: instead, advocate good, nutrient-dense, dietary carb sources. Reserving 'sports drinks' for competition, and highlighting the risks of impaired energy-regulation, tooth decay and weight gain, would seem to be a sensible approach to these products.

under-consumption. Your client may well not know that too much water can tax their kidneys, contribute to digestive disorders, and lead to mineral depletion and electrolyte imbalances.

It is probably best, and safest, to talk to clients and pupils in general terms about adequate hydration. As a guide, they are probably adequately hydrated if they rarely experience thirst, and their urine is colourless or slightly yellow. (This will at least get the kids giggling.) Signs of dehydration can include a dry mouth, headaches, light-headedness, dark or scanty urine, and constipation (giggles again). Drinks containing caffeine or alcohol can increase fluid output, making it more difficult to stay adequately hydrated.

A good way to determine individual requirements is to weigh the client before and after training. Weight loss in kilos is equivalent to litres of water lost. They should aim to minimise this weight loss by drinking throughout the session – or drinking 1.5 x sweat loss in order to replace fluids and compensate for continued sweating after the workout. They should sip little and often, no matter how thirsty they may feel. If they 'guzzle' their water, this can make them feel bloated and very uncomfortable. Make sure they get into the habit of arriving at each session well hydrated, bringing their preferred water or sports drink with them and continuing to hydrate after their workouts.

DIET AND ALCOHOL

Alcohol is not classed as a nutrient, but the body can burn it as a source of energy. As well as being aware of the negative health implications of alcohol consumption, it is important for your clients to be familiar with the following facts.

Unlike carbohydrate, protein and fat – which pass through the stomach into the small intestine before being absorbed into the bloodstream – alcohol passes directly through the stomach's lining. It therefore arrives in the blood 'first', and will be used in preference to key nutrients, as fuel for the body's activities.

Explain to your client what this means in practical terms. While their body is using up the alcohol that is available in their bloodstream, the good-quality food they have eaten as part of their balanced diet – the one that the pair of you have discussed and agreed upon – is being overlooked. Depending on how much alcohol they have consumed, these good nutrients may be treated like any other form of excess energy, and either excreted or stored in the tissues as body fat. And this can continue for some time after the client has stopped drinking – even into the following day!

Of course this doesn't mean you should be a hard-assed fitness trainer who forbids your client from enjoying a glass or wine, or a beer. After all, if they are generally eating well and exercising hard, they should be able to have a treat. But they should also bear the above in mind, and remember to keep an extra-close eye on what and how much they are eating if they are consuming alcohol.

If you have a client who persists in drinking what you consider to be too much during their boxing fitness programme, try pointing out to them that all their sweat, fatigue and indeed money is pretty much going to waste. If they are in a dehydrated, hungover state, their training will suffer – quite apart from the fact that they will feel awful while they're doing it.

It is very hard to remain motivated in your work if you feel that everything you are putting into someone's workouts is being undone down the pub. At some point, you may need to balance whether you wish to retain them as a client, or whether your time and effort would be better spent elsewhere. Whatever you do, never, ever train someone who turns up to a session under the influence of alcohol. Your insurance will be invalid; your professional reputation on the line; their techniques seriously compromised; and their risk of injury significantly increased.

INJURY PREVENTION // AND TREATMENT

19

By definition, boxing fitness is a very safe workout. Glove-to-body contact – the potentially dangerous element of boxing – has been entirely removed from the equation, so that as long as you follow all the health and safety practices expected of the qualified exercise professional, it is highly unlikely that you or your clients will get hurt.

As covered in detail in Parts One and Two of this *Complete Guide*, you will safeguard everyone concerned if you:

- Are appropriately covered by the necessary professional, legislative and insurance covenants. Review these regularly, and keep them current.
- Choose a suitable training venue or location for every client or group, and check it for potential hazards – thoroughly, and on an ongoing basis.
- Make sure there is adequate first-aid equipment close at hand, or carry your own basic kit with you in your gym bag.
- Check each client's state of health – mind and body – and don't take anyone through the training if you are not happy that they are well and engaged.
- Fully brief your clients and pupils as to the appropriate clothing and footwear for their sessions. Don't let anyone work out if they are inappropriately dressed.
- Ensure that no client or pupil eats while training, but that all are adequately hydrated. Dehydration can make them lose focus and impair coordination, making it more likely that they might injure themselves.
- Wrap everyone's hands well.
- Make sure everyone warms up and cools down thoroughly, towels off excess sweat, and puts on dry clothes at the end of every session.

Perhaps the most important safety consideration, however, is technique. As has been emphasised throughout this book, good technique is fundamental to safe and effective boxing training – and therefore to injury prevention.

When you are learning to box, work hard on your own technique. When you are teaching, be stringent about the important things: good stance; strong wrists and straight contact with the knuckles in the shots and combinations… you know the score. You can always recap on the key teaching points, checking back through this book at any time. Never think you have it all mastered: even the most seasoned professional boxers continue to hone and improve their technical skills throughout their careers.

SOME POTENTIAL BOXING-RELATED INJURIES AND AILMENTS
DELAYED ONSET MUSCLE SORENESS (DOMS)

DOMS – the gradually increasing, post-exercise muscle soreness that sets in between 24 and 48 hours after a workout – is by far the most likely complaint your clients will suffer from as a result of boxing fitness. You will know that this training effect is perfectly normal, and nothing to worry about; however, it can be quite alarming for people who have not experienced it before.

Because DOMS is usually the result of unaccustomed physical activity, for clients or pupils who haven't previously boxed it is almost inevitable that they will be afflicted in the early days of their programme. The main culprit is the eccentric contraction of their muscles when punching: this stresses the tissue beyond what it is used to, resulting in microscopic tears in the muscle fibres accompanied by inflammation.

The important thing is to *warn novice clients what to expect*. If they know that anyone can get DOMS, and that it is an indication of positive adaptations occurring in their muscles – making them stronger and better able to perform the workout next time – they won't be so worried or reluctant to continue with their training when the soreness subsides.

As you'll be aware, there's not that much to be done to alleviate the pain of DOMS. Rest, ice, heat and stretching can be helpful to the process of recovery. If your client is really suffering, suggest that they take it easy for a few days, or try some light, un-boxing-related activity such as walking or swimming. Make sure you include an especially thorough cool-down phase in everyone's first few boxing fitness workouts, as this can assist in preventing the worst of the soreness. Telling them (quite genuinely) that it's never going to be quite as bad again can also be a big help!

Make sure you are able to differentiate between general DOMS and particular muscle overuse or injury. If the pain is localised, acute and/or lasts for more than around 72 hours, further investigation may be necessary by an appropriate professional.

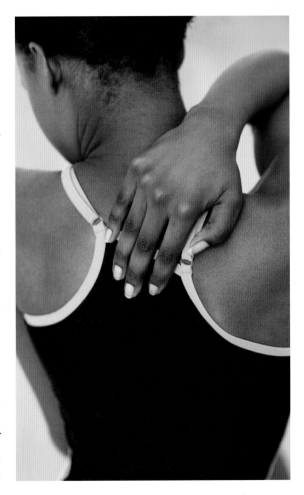

SOFT TISSUE INJURY/INFLAMMATION

Because boxing fitness is a safe, non-contact type of training, injuries or ailments tend to be restricted to minor soft-tissue injuries or inflammation – affecting muscles, tendons and fascia, rather than bones or joints. When such problems do occur, they are most likely to affect your clients' arms, wrists and hands as a result of repeated punching against the resistant surface of punch bag or focus pads. Incorrect or poor boxing technique can cause or exacerbate the condition.

If your client is getting sore shoulders, hands or wrists, it may be advisable to stop their sessions for a while and tell them to rest. Depending on where and how bad the pain is, you could continue with shadow boxing, footwork, skipping and/or core strength and stability training, omitting only the bag and focus pad work that is at the root of the pain and inflammation. Discuss the problem with them, and take a view. To reduce the inflammatory response, explain or show them how to ice the affected area. Make sure they place any ice used in a towel before applying it, to protect the skin.

If the affected area swells up, use compression. Your first aid course will have taught you how to apply an elastic bandage to maintain healthy blood flow in the limb; the bandage should fit snugly but not be too tight. Encourage them, if possible, to elevate the limb in order to limit swelling and aid the removal of waste products from the problem area. They can safely resume training as soon as they are pain-free.

Be wary of recommending the use of particular anti-inflammatory medications, in case your client has an adverse response to these. If you feel they may be necessary, always recommend that the advice of a pharmacist be sought before purchase. As with any injury or illness, if you're not sure about the cause or the best way in which to proceed with treatment, recommend that they pay a visit to their doctor.

BLISTERS

Chafing and blisters may occur in boxing when the delicate skin of the hands, especially the area over the knuckles, is subjected to repeated friction. Keep an eye on your clients' hands and limit their punch bag and focus pad work if you see redness or soreness developing. Don't let them continue punching until the skin is broken and/or bleeding: by then it's too late, and your client will need to wait for the area to heal before resuming bag or pad work. If they don't rest the hands, the skin will simply keep on opening up, with an attendant risk of infection.

If blisters do occur, the area should be kept clean and dry. There is conflicting advice as to whether plasters should be worn to promote healing and prevent infection: they are generally recommended these days, but if you are unsure or concerned, a doctor should be consulted. It's always best to prevent the blisters in the first place by wrapping clients' hands well and, where possible, choosing to work them out on a punch bag that isn't too 'tight' or firm. Remember that you can also bind half an ordinary bathroom sponge over their knuckles on each hand, underneath the hand-wraps, to provide extra cushioning.

PAIN IN THE FEET/ANKLES/KNEES FROM SKIPPING

This can sometimes occur, because skipping is a high-impact activity. You will already have advised your clients to wear well-cushioned trainers rather than boxing boots, and to skip on a floor surface that is neither unyielding nor too soft or unstable.

If such precautions don't prevent or help with pain in the lower limb, you should either omit skipping from their sessions altogether (working on their stamina with alternative cardio-based activities, and on their speed, balance and coordination with lots of footwork and quick punching combinations), or limit it to short, light intervals. Gradually build these up as the structures surrounding and supporting the feet, ankles and knees become stronger.

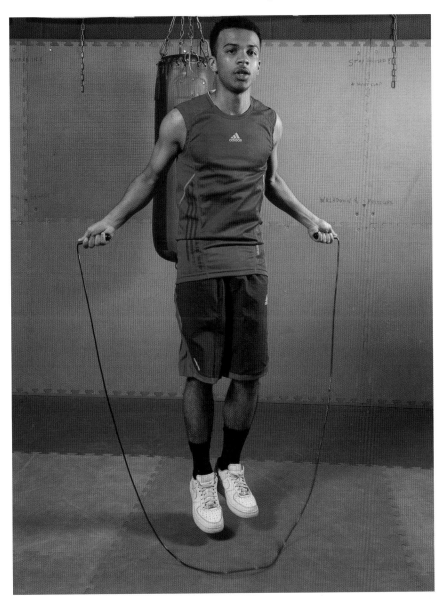

Skipping is an impact activity: to avoid lower limb pain, choose a suitable floor surface and supportive footwear.

OTHER HEALTH CONSIDERATIONS

20

As part of your professional training and qualifications, you will have considered what are termed 'special populations': for example, those aged under 18; the elderly; women during pregnancy and post-childbirth; and people who have been diagnosed with a pre-existing disease or medical condition, such as coronary heart disease, diabetes or asthma. You will have been given guidance as to what precautions may be necessary for each group, to ensure that they undertake appropriate fitness training and remain safe and well while doing so.

It is not within the scope of this *Complete Guide* to cover special populations and boxing fitness in any great detail. Nor is it in fact strictly necessary, because no particular contra-indications apply to boxing training that do not also apply to other sports and types of fitness activity. If you adhere to the same guidelines you would follow for any kind of personal training, sports coaching or PE teaching, and always consult a medical or other relevant professional if you are in any doubt about the suitability of an exercise or workout for your client, you won't go far wrong.

Having said that, here are a few comments that may help.

CHILDREN AND YOUNG ADULTS

Young people can benefit hugely from boxing fitness training. Not only do they find it enjoyable, but it also gives them a safe and controlled environment in which to use up their energy, and to channel any anger or frustration they may be feeling. Learning how to 'handle oneself' is an important part of every youngster's education. Boxing, as a sport and as a fitness activity, is an ideal way in which to teach them the discipline, focus and self-control they will need in their daily lives.

Since health and wellbeing are so closely inter-linked, there is a further, relevant dimension to this. For many young adults today, boxing clubs and gyms offer opportunities for sporting and social inclusion that may not exist for them elsewhere. It has been shown that young people who are harder to reach through more mainstream channels; who may have dropped out of the education system; and who are therefore vulnerable and at risk of turning to crime or violence, welcome boxing as a physical and emotional outlet.

From the age of 11, youngsters have the option of training to compete in the sport of amateur boxing. This, in the UK, falls under the auspices of the Amateur Boxing Association (ABA, www.abae.co.uk); other national governing bodies and local/regional divisions can be contacted via the International Boxing Association (AIBA, www.aiba.org). As mentioned early in this book, amateur boxers wear protective headgear, and the sport is subject to stringent safety measures to protect its participants.

If you are teaching any young people, male or female, who may wish to join an amateur boxing club, help them research a club near to them that is fully affiliated to the appropriate divisional arm of the sport's governing body. Ensure too that the rules and regulations are carefully adhered to by the coaches and management. It is your responsibility as the referring exercise professional, as well as the responsibility of the club, to ensure a young person's health, safety and welfare.

You will already know that although there are no barriers to exercise for most healthy youngsters, the lifting of heavy weights should be avoided until an individual has reached his or her full growth potential. Any resistance work undertaken as part of a conditioning programme should be limited to the young person's bodyweight: bones, muscles and joints in the growing body must not be put under undue stress if they are to develop fully and healthily.

THE OLDER PRACTITIONER

Older people may suffer from a number of diseases associated with the ageing process, including cardiovascular diseases, e.g. coronary heart disease and high blood pressure; musculo-skeletal diseases, e.g. osteoporosis (brittle bones) and certain types of arthritis; respiratory diseases, e.g. asthma; metabolic diseases, e.g. diabetes and obesity; and neurological diseases, e.g. Parkinson's and Alzheimer's.

Even if your clients do not suffer from any of these conditions, certain negative changes in their anatomy and physiology are unavoidable as they age – such as loss of bone density, decreased range of movement in the joints, increased body fat, and

a decline in postural control. For these and other reasons, you will always recommend that an older adult (from the age of 40 upwards) seeks clearance and/or advice from a qualified medical professional before embarking on any unaccustomed exercise programme.

Reassure the older practitioner that if there are no health indications to the contrary, boxing fitness – being flexible and easily matched to each individual's requirements – is perfect for introducing an appropriate programme of physical activity, and for increasing this in suitable, incremental ways. Remind them of the many benefits of exercise, which include reduced body fat and increased lean tissue mass; increased bone and muscle strength; improved mobility, posture and balance; enhanced cardiorespiratory function; and emotional and mental wellbeing.

PREGNANCY AND POST-CHILDBIRTH

As long as your client is well, and has been relatively active both prior to and during her pregnancy, there is no reason for her not to undertake a carefully considered boxing fitness programme.

Encourage her by explaining that the workouts will:

- Help burn off excess calories, making post-labour slimming and toning much easier.
- Improve blood flow, alleviating some of the typical pregnancy-related discomforts such as fluid retention and swollen joints.
- Enhance muscle strength and endurance, aiding the birth process and reducing physical fatigue post-labour, when she is doing all the hard work of carrying the baby together with extensive equipment!

- Increase endorphin levels, aiding with stress, anxiety management, and insomnia.
- Boost her confidence, as she looks healthier and happier with an enviable maternal 'bloom'.

Keep a careful eye on your client's blood pressure throughout her programme. Tailor the sessions to avoid impact activity such as skipping, and build in more core stability exercises to help maintain good posture, both as her pregnancy bump grows, and after the baby is born.

Talk to her about the particular importance of adequate hydration during pregnancy and breast-feeding, and take extra care, when leading her warm-up and cool-down stretches, that she keeps within the normal joint range of motion, thus taking into account any potential joint instability caused by the action of the pregnancy hormone *relaxin*.

Finally, stress that good communication between client and trainer is essential during this period. If she should experience any faintness, dizziness, pain or other abnormal symptoms as a result of her boxing fitness workouts, she must tell you immediately. You will then recommend a full medical check-up, at the earliest possible opportunity.

5

PART **FIVE**

PARTNER, GROUP AND CONDITIONING TRAINING

PARTNER AND GROUP TRAINING

21

Depending on a number of variables – for example, your preference and that of your employer/client(s); venue type and size; availability or lack of equipment; and questions of cost – you may conduct training sessions one-on-one, in small groups of two or more, or as a full-sized class. Boxing fitness is sufficiently flexible to accommodate all of these options, as long as you plan the workout carefully to make sure it is safe and effective for each and every participant.

As a self-employed fitness professional, even if you keep your hourly rates as reasonable as possible, some prospective clients may find the cost of individual personal training prohibitive. The good news is that boxing fitness is ideally suited to those wishing to share sessions with a partner or with friends, making the activity more affordable for them while keeping the demands upon you within reasonable limits. In fact, shared sessions can be good news for the trainer too, since each person may be able and willing to pay a little more than their proportional share of your hourly fee. In this way you end up with a bit of a 'bonus', which is fair enough; there is additional work involved in planning sessions and programmes for multiple participants, and possibly more investment on your part in such things as equipment

and laundry. As long as you bear in mind the cost/value ratio for you and your clients, everyone can benefit from shared workouts.

You may find that everyone you train wants to work on the focus pads, for as often and as long as possible. As has been discussed earlier in this book, focus pad training is the closest most people will ever come to 'real' boxing, and for this reason alone they will probably love it. In shared and group sessions, you therefore need to consider your own ability to manage more than one person on the pads. This is important, not just in terms of your physical resources and the progressive wear and tear on your joints, but also in terms of organisation. To ensure that each participant works hard enough, and is sufficiently stimulated, for the full hour's duration, it is paramount to structure your workouts accordingly. If circumstances dictate that the emphasis of any particular session is on the focus pads, with more than two or possibly three participants you're likely to struggle to keep everyone warm, engaged and occupied.

WITH TWO CLIENTS...

Of course, the more creative you can be in such situations, the better. With two relatively unfit clients, you might think up a repertoire of drills on the pads that you can practise with each person in turn, while the other recovers. This can be hard work for the trainer, who gets no rest, but makes for a fun and effective workout with interaction between all three of you, and with both clients learning from watching the other. Here is an example:

- After an appropriate warm-up, and with both clients wearing hand-wraps and gloves, get them to stand facing each other with you positioned in between. Make sure they don't stand too close: you need enough room to be able to turn through 180 degrees towards each person as they perform their drills, and for them to be able to punch at full extension with correct technique.

- Client A performs the first drill – e.g. 10 x double jab-cross/back hand – with Client B watching. As A recovers, you turn towards B, who repeats the same drill.

- Continue alternating your chosen drills in this way, selecting from the exercises suggested on page 102 or devising your own. You might repeat the whole repertoire several times, with a minute's rest between each 'set' (your arms and shoulders will need a break), by way of a mini circuit.

Figure 21.1 Taking two clients on the focus pads.

• Depending on your clients' fitness level and the aim of the session, you may then wish to add some continuous punching. You could get B to time A – for 30 seconds, or a minute – before they swap round. Or, if both clients are quite fit and you don't want either of them standing idle while the other works, get them to punch simultaneously, one on each focus pad as shown in Figure 21.2. As has been pointed out already in this book, hitting a single pad continuously (*one-two-one-two-one-two*) is very good cardio and core work.

As your clients become fitter, you may need to up the ante by devising a way in which one can continue working while the other hits the pads. Use your imagination to keep the 'spare' client on their toes. Introduce some squats: B performs body-weight squats in sets of ten, with ten seconds in between, while A is punching. Then press-ups (yes, they can do them wearing boxing gloves), and/or sit-ups, and/or shadow boxing – they might copy the drills you are doing with A, without the target.

If you have access to a heavy bag, alternate bag and pad work between the two of them. Or

Figure 21.2 One client on each focus pad.

Figure 21.3 For fitter clients – one skips while the other does pads, before swapping over.

introduce the skipping rope: B skips for a two- or three-minute round as you are working on the pads with A; all of you take a minute's rest before A and B swap round. There are plenty of ways you can provide a fun and effective session with two clients simultaneously: just use your imagination, and don't be scared to try new things.

WITH THREE CLIENTS...

With three clients, you have additional options. While you are working on the focus pads with Client A, Clients B and C partner up. They should be wearing hand-wraps, but not boxing gloves, and facing each other in their stance. First,

they might practise the drills suggested on page 102, taking it in turns to:

- Use their lead hand to touch the other person's body, with their partner taking evasive action until 'tagged', at which point they swap around;
- Attempt to touch their partner's front foot with their own, with the partner moving their feet quickly to get out of the way – again, swapping once they have made contact.

Even though you are busy with A, try to keep an eye on the pair as best you can, perhaps calling out 'Switch!' at set or random intervals, and

Figure 21.4 Push-of-war partner drill.

suggesting any necessary corrections to their stance or reminding them to keep their hands up.

Then, introduce some new partnered activities. Here are a couple of ideas; try these, or think up your own:

• *Push-of-war*: a great exercise for isometric strength and stability in the boxing stance (see figure 21.4). Get B and C to place their hands on each other's shoulders – remaining in their stance – and on 'Go!' to try to push each other backwards, both doing their utmost to resist being forced out of position. They should maintain their efforts for, say, 30 seconds, before relaxing and then trying again. You could introduce a forfeit for the person who gives way first (ten press-ups, or sit-ups) or, if the pair's respective bodyweights make

Figure 21.5 Piston arms partner drill.

the exercise a bit unfair, handicap the stronger/heavier one – perhaps with one hand held behind their back, the pushing hand centred on their partner's torso rather than on one shoulder, to help keep the pair balanced.

- *Piston arms*: very effective in building punching speed and muscular endurance. In their stance, instruct B and C to hold hands as shown in figure 21.5 and then, as fast as possible, to 'piston' their arms alternately *in-out-in-out*. It's a little like replicating the movement of continuous punching, but joined together in a kind of speed race. They should maintain their shared efforts over a set period of time, rest, and then begin again.

As well as devising your own partnered exercises for B and C to do while you are working with A, get the pair to practise the boxing defence drills described in Chapter 12. Not only does each of these defences have at least one specific fitness benefit, but they will also stand your clients in good stead should they ever wish to progress to contact sparring or to competition (see also pages 151–5).

For defence drills, both partners should wear wraps under sparring gloves, and take it in turn to duck, slip, roll under, block, parry and push away from their partner's jab. Obviously, stress that the jab is non-contact: the pair should stand sufficiently close that they can respond realistically to an 'attacking shot', but far enough apart to avoid any kind of forceful touch. Depending on their level of fitness and experience, you can also build in footwork and counterpunching (see pages 36–41 and 74 respectively). Always try to keep an eye on what they're doing and, if you're giving Client A some breathing space, take a

little time to demonstrate key teaching points or make corrections to the pair's technique. Factor in plenty of verbal encouragement, so they know they're not being neglected.

Obviously, rotate the three clients in turn so that each of them has the same amount of individual attention on the focus pads. If you have skipping ropes and sufficient space, you might structure an hour's boxing fitness session like this:

- Warm-up (pulse-raiser and stretching)
- Client A – 3 minutes' focus pads while B and C do partner drills
- Client B – 3 minutes' focus pads while A and C skip
- Client C – 3 minutes' focus pads while A and B do partner drills
- *3 minutes' rest for everyone, for towelling off and hydration*

Figure 21.6 Practising defence drills – safely.

- Client A – 3 minutes' focus pads while B and C skip
- Client B – 3 minutes' focus pads while A and C do partner drills
- Client C – 3 minutes' focus pads while A and B skip
- Repeat
- Core work and/or conditioning for all
- Warm-down

You'll see that each person does the same amount of work, both partnered and individually, during the hour, with plenty of variety built in and a good mix of cardio, strength and core stability training. Such a session is quite hard work for the trainer, so make sure you pace your pad work accordingly.

If you have access to a heavy bag, you can choose to replace the second or the third 'set' of focus pad rounds by bag work, to reduce the stress on your wrists and shoulders. When you've done a few similar sessions with three clients, you'll understand why it's not really possible to train a larger group in this way: workouts for four or more participants need to be undertaken differently, as discussed below.

WORKING WITH LARGER GROUPS

If you are employed by a gym or fitness centre, or work with schools and other organisations, you may be required to teach boxing fitness to larger classes, comprised of varying numbers of

Figure 21.7 Shadow boxing with a group.

participants of different ages, abilities and fitness levels. This can be quite a challenge but, with good organisational skills, firm discipline and creative ideas, it is entirely possible to deliver effective and progressive group sessions and programmes.

In terms of equipment, we have already covered the minimum requirement for each participant: a towel, some fresh water, a skipping rope, a pair of hand-wraps and some boxing gloves. You yourself simply need a method of timing rounds, and your focus pads.

The training venue may be a gym, studio, school or church hall, or an outdoor space. As advised on page 12, do your due diligence in respect of all venue and personal health and safety concerns. Encourage participants to wrap their own or a partner's hands as efficiently as possible in order to take up the least amount of class time. If they have their own wraps, they could even arrive at the venue with their hands already prepared. Most important of all, make sure there is enough space for people to punch out, practise their footwork and skip without hitting or otherwise interfering with their neighbours. For bigger classes, it's unlikely that there will be room for everyone to skip simultaneously, so you may need to split the group into 'stations' and move people around after a set period of time.

How technical you make your boxing fitness classes is up to you. You will obviously want to cover the basic techniques – stance, guard, straight punches and simple footwork – and to find a way of doing so that holds people's attention. Unless your group is very fit and experienced, there's no need to progress too quickly (if at all) onto more complex boxing skills, since you can work any kind of class harder by increasing the intensity or duration of their efforts, and/or reducing recovery time.

When teaching the basics, stand at the front of the class and use your tried-and-tested combination of 'show and tell' – explaining *and* demonstrating the key points for each technique, perhaps from a variety of angles to make sure that everyone in the class can see you. Then get them to practise, calling out plenty of instructions and encouragement:

'Now show me your best jabs! Remember, you *always* jab with your lead hand, whether that's the left for orthodox or the right for southpaw. Throw those jabs straight out and straight back, snapping the hand back into the guard position – don't drop it down: if you were in the ring that'd be "good night, see you tomorrow"! Great, much better. Again: jab, jab, now double it up – good!'

As they practise each technique, move around the group giving some feedback. You might hold up a palm, or one of your focus pads, for each person to hit in turn, so they get the feel of what it's like to punch against a target, and you can show them how the knuckled part of their fist makes the contact (although if your group is shadow boxing, wearing wraps alone, remind them to hit softly, or they risk hurting themselves – or you).

Use your judgement as to when people's attention is wandering and it's time to move on to the next skill. You can't afford to spend too much time correcting individuals, so from the outset keep your instructions to the group clear and concise, repeat the key teaching points, and only pick up on things that are glaringly wrong or dangerous to a particular participant or their classmates. It will really help the flow of any class if you are dynamic and purposeful, with a clear idea of where things are moving to next. Once people start wandering around or chatting, it's quite hard to get them back on track.

While covering the basic techniques with the group working together, it's a good idea to try to identify those who are grasping things well and those who might be struggling, as well as those who have obviously done some boxing-related activity versus those who are complete novices. If you can pair or group people in your mind in reasonably homogenous combinations, it makes things simpler when it comes to breaking up the class into smaller units of a similar standard. Similarly, consider height and bodyweight, as well as stance. You don't want to pair a really tall, skinny southpaw against a short, weighty orthodox for partner drills if you don't have to! Keep things as simple as possible for you, and for them.

In terms of how you might structure an hour-long session for a larger class, this needn't differ too much from how you would organise a small group (see above), or even individual training. The base session remains the same:

- Pulse-raiser
- Stretching and mobility work
- Shadow boxing
- Heavy bag work (if available)
- Skipping
- Focus pad work
- Core stability and conditioning work
- Warm-down

The main distinction will be in how much focus pad work you are able to factor in. After some rounds of group shadow boxing, for example, you might pair people up:

'Everyone, find a partner who is roughly your height and weight, and if possible who works out of the same stance as you – quick as you can. Anyone left without a partner can work in a three, or with me.'

Give each pair a number, and then instruct all even-numbered pairs to skip while all odd-numbered pairs do partner drills. You then take each pair in turn, starting at 1, and work on the pads with them until everyone has had a go. Half-way through, you instruct the even- and odd-numbered pairs to swap activities.

Or, you might split a class of 20 participants into four groups: Group 1 skips; Group 2 does a mini-circuit, set beforehand or written on a board; Group 3 works on the heavy bag; and Group 4 comes to you for pad work. There are no set rules. You need to try out your ideas, refine what works and discard what doesn't, and make some creative, progressive changes as people's fitness and ability levels improve. Once you are confident with larger groups of clients, class work can be really fun for you, as well as for them.

CORE WORK AND CONDITIONING

22

BOXING AND THE CORE

As every exercise professional knows, developing good core strength and stability is important, not only to optimise performance in a range of sports, but also to promote everyday functional fitness.

Sometimes misrepresented as involving only the abdominal muscles, the 'core' of the human body in fact comprises the superficial and deep spinal extensors, all the abdominals, the pelvic floor muscles, and the muscles of the hip and shoulder girdle – everything, in short, that serves to keep the trunk upright and in alignment. A strong, stable core facilitates a 'neutral' spine with healthy natural curvature. This in turn enables good posture, thereby reducing muscle fatigue and the likelihood of injury, especially to the neck, shoulders and back.

The actions involved in boxing training both require and develop good core strength and stability. As has been discussed elsewhere in this book, it's not possible to deliver effective punches and combinations with the arms alone: the whole body – feet, legs, hips, torso, arms and shoulders – must be involved in order to maintain balance and achieve power and accuracy. The hook in particular depends on rotation around a strong, stable core; even a grounded stance should engage the muscles of the trunk. A boxing fitness session, done well, is a total body workout.

For this reason, as long as your clients are practising their boxing fitness with correct technique, their core strength and stability will gradually improve. Positive adaptations in the core muscles will be reflected in any sporting or everyday activity that requires lifting, turning, balance and coordination, as well as in the client's general posture and body shape. This will happen as a natural by-product of their training, without the need to focus on specific core strength and conditioning exercises.

This is great, but also requires caution on your part with clients who are new to boxing training, and especially those who have a history of spinal injury or back pain. You will already have advised such individuals to obtain clearance by a qualified doctor before starting their programme. Nothing should therefore go amiss, as long as the positive fitness adaptations are allowed to take place slowly, without causing undue stress on the spinal structures. As the clients' core muscles become stronger, any vulnerability in the area of the back should improve significantly.

Remember to reassure all novice clients that unfamiliar exercise will almost inevitably incur

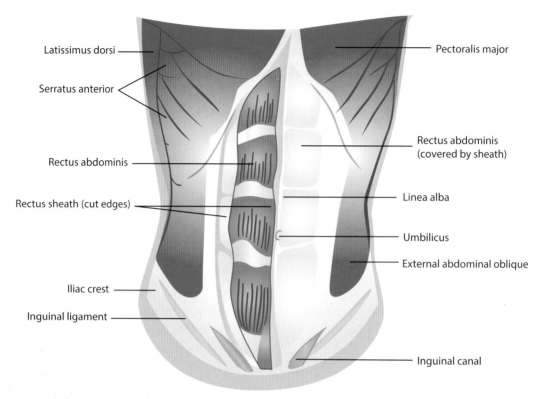

Latissimus dorsi

Serratus anterior

Rectus abdominis

Rectus sheath (cut edges)

Iliac crest

Inguinal ligament

Pectoralis major

Rectus abdominis (covered by sheath)

Linea alba

Umbilicus

External abdominal oblique

Inguinal canal

Figure 22.1 The muscles of the core.

some muscle soreness (see DOMS, pages 125–6), and boxing is no exception. After their first few sessions, they are likely to discover muscles they didn't know existed, particularly in the arms, shoulders and back. If the soreness persists, or if you or they are concerned about its nature, hold off the training and arrange a check-up with a medical professional.

SPECIFIC CORE TRAINING USING BOXING TECHNIQUES

While it's true that general improvements in core strength and stability are a by-product of boxing training, it's also advisable to build some specific core exercises into your clients' sessions

– given that the stronger and more stable this area of the body, the more effective their boxing techniques will be. In addition, many individuals wish to focus on toning and strengthening their 'abs', and with a little imagination you can address this in fun and engaging ways during a boxing fitness session.

Some focus pad drills for the core have already been recommended in Chapter 17, and with a little creativity you can think up your own. For example, consider combining punching with Swiss ball work. Swiss ball exercises are a great contribution to any personal training programme, and if you're a mobile PT with a car (into which you can safely fit an inflated ball), take one along with you to the park or to your client's house to add some scope to your core exercise repertoire.

As part of your professional qualification you will have learned a number of such exercises – such as a Swiss ball sit-up, illustrated in figure 22.2.

- Your client lies on the ball as shown, making sure their neck and upper back are supported. Their feet should be firmly planted on the floor, knees at a 90-degree angle and hips up level with the rest of their body – don't let their pelvis 'sag' so they are sitting 'into' the ball. Instruct them to hold their core in tightly and concentrate on the area just below their tummy button.

- Instruct them to contract their core muscles, at the same time lifting their head and shoulders from the ball in a small sit-up. They hold at the top of the movement, then slowly lower: this is one rep.

To make this basic sit-up boxing-specific, why not try incorporating some focus pad work? Here is one suggestion, illustrated in figure 22.3.

Figure 22.2 Swiss ball sit-up.

Figure 22.3 Swiss ball sit-up with punching.

- With your focus pads, stand in front of the ball. (Depending on the floor surface, and your client's preference, you may need to use your feet as a 'block' to stop theirs from slipping, or even tread lightly on the toes of their trainers to anchor them in place. Try not to over-do this support, however, or it will be the client's hip flexors, rather than their abs, that do most of the work. If you prefer, you can also perform this exercise kneeling so you don't have to bend or lean over. In this case, your knees will provide the block or anchor.)
- Hold the pads out in front of you, judging the distance so that when the client sits up and punches, they will be able to do so with the correct reach and technique.
- Then, instruct the client to sit up, all the while pulling their core in tightly, and to punch the pads (see figure 22.3): one repetition will be when they sit up, punch the pads, then return to the start position.
- It's up to you what punch combinations you ask for. You might try three sets of 10 x sit up followed by one-two, or by four straight, or by left hook-right hook, or even by some short-ened uppercuts. Or a combination of these. The point is that by incorporating boxing techniques into the exercise, more of the core muscles are engaged for longer – thus making the work much more effective.

Of course, if you don't have a Swiss ball, the exercise described above can be done with the client simply lying face-up on a mat on the floor, with their feet flat and knees bent. You kneel at their feet and hold the pads just above their knees, so that as they sit up they can perform the required punches and combinations.

With or without the Swiss ball, think later-ally and devise your own variations on the 'boxing sit-up'. Try asking the client to sit up, punch both pads simultaneously (as if pushing you away) x 10 before lying back down and repeating a set number of times.

Or, with your client lying on the floor, stand astride them with one foot on the floor either side of their waist. Then bend at the waist and hold the pads horizontally, as if for an uppercut, and instruct them to punch straight *up* – into the air from their supine position, *one-two-one-two-one-two*, as many times as you see fit. If you feel like being especially devious, gradually move the pads higher so they have to stretch in order to make contact.

All these types of exercise, however 'wacky' they may seem (no pun intended), are fun and work the core muscles. Don't be scared of trying something new, as long as you're sure it's safe. And whatever core-specific work you do with your client, don't forget to balance abdominal exercises with some that are designed to improve lower back strength and flexibility.

GENERAL CONDITIONING FOR IMPROVED BOXING PERFORMANCE

The fitter your clients, the more scope you have to be creative in devising a progressive boxing train-ing programme that is tailor-made to meet their goals. As you will already know, how often a person can exercise – and exercise with you – depends on a number of different factors, including their personal motivation, the time they have available, the state of their health, and the money they are able to spend.

If you are working with groups or classes, members may meet only once a week; this can also be the case for private clients, who need to schedule sessions into their (and your) busy timetable, and are perhaps unable to afford more than one supervised workout a week.

This can be frustrating, since ideally you will be advising your clients to work out at least three times per week. Once, or even twice, will keep them heart-healthy and 'ticking over', but if they want to see significant improvements in their fitness – however they may define their goals (see also pages 20–1) – they are likely to need to do some training on their own to supplement the boxing sessions they are enjoying with you.

Although your clients can't work on the focus pads in your absence, they will be able to undertake some or all of the other boxing fitness elements described in this book. If you are setting them unsupervised sessions, consider incorporating a number of rounds of shadow boxing, skipping and punch bag work, appropriate in number and intensity to the stage they are at in their programme. Finish with a good range of core exercises, making sure beforehand that they are familiar with the correct techniques.

When writing your clients' sessions, be careful to provide sufficient detail to guide them through a solo workout, since this will help give them structure and focus when you're not there. Particularly with novices, telling them to 'do three rounds of shadow boxing' is too vague. Instead, establish exactly how these should be broken down, perhaps as follows:

Round 1:
- 60 seconds of straight punches
- 60 seconds of hooks and uppercuts
- 60 seconds of footwork
- *Rest for 60 seconds*

Round 2:
- 60 seconds practising all the punches and combinations
- 60 seconds of footwork
- 60 seconds combining punches, combinations and footwork
- *Rest for 60 seconds*

Round 3:
- 60 seconds of defence techniques
- 60 seconds of footwork
- 60 seconds of defence and footwork combined

If you think the client will benefit from some cross-training between their boxing sessions, you might set resistance work such as free or machine weights, swimming or cycling, all of which will improve their strength and stamina, thus enhancing their performance and recovery during their time with you.

Bear in mind that boxing is basically interval training – bouts of intense work over fixed time periods (rounds), interspersed with set periods of rest. Therefore, to achieve synergy between your clients' conditioning work and their boxing-specific training, consider structuring the majority of their cardio efforts in the same way. On the exercise bike, for example, instead of asking for 15 minutes of steady-state work, break this down into e.g. 5 x 2 minutes' hard effort with one minute of easy cycling in between. It's always good to set the recovery period at 60 seconds, since this is the fixed rest time between rounds of boxing training, sparring and competition.

RUNNING OR 'ROADWORK'
Running – 'roadwork' – is an integral part of every boxer's workout regime. Depending on the

training phase they are in, they will undertake a combination of steady-state (long, slow) runs, and interval training such as hills and sprints. Roadwork builds stamina, facilitating the boxer's recovery between rounds of sparring and competition, as well as improving their speed, strength and power in the ring. It is also an important part of their mental preparation, requiring both focus and dedication.

Because running and boxing are such complementary activities, you may well encourage your clients to do some roadwork between their boxing fitness sessions. If they are limited as to the number of PT sessions they are able to undertake in a week, it makes sense for them to do their technical work with you, especially on the focus pads, and to run by themselves when they can schedule it in.

When setting a solo running session for a client, be sure to specify the details of the required effort. Those not used to roadwork can be daunted by the prospect of, say, a 20-minute run, so instead try

breaking it down into something more physically and psychologically manageable. For example, you might write the session as follows:

- Easy walking: 1–2 minutes
- Power walking: 2 minutes
- Jogging: 5 minutes
- Fast striding: 5 x 30 seconds (1 minute recovery between each rep)
- Easy jogging to finish
- Stretch

With this type of workout – in fact, with any solo cardio activity – encourage the client to consider the 'shape' of their session. You might even draw it as a graph on their programme card, with time along the bottom, and intensity along the vertical axis. (The intensity can be expressed as a readily recognisable effort, as above; as a percentage of maximal effort, e.g. 50%; or as an RPE value/range – see below.) If the client is focusing on structuring their run according to your requirements, and on performing defined work levels and recovery periods, they will be less concerned with the pain!

To communicate the effort intensity you require when you're not there to supervise a conditioning session, it's useful to refer to the RPE scale – standing for Rating of Perceived Exertion – also known as the Borg scale. You may well have learned about this as part of your professional qualification, but here's a quick recap.

The scale generally runs from 6 to 20, with 6 being minimal exertion, and 20 being maximal effort. At an RPE range of 6–8, your client will be exercising very lightly. At 8–10 they will feel flushed and a little out of breath, and at 10–12 they will experience mild discomfort. At 12–14, they really wouldn't want to be holding a conversation; the work is quite hard, and they have to focus in order to continue. Above 16, and the exercise is very strenuous; your client will feel very tired and really need to push themselves to complete the task.

If you explain this method to a client before they go out on a solo session, it becomes easier for you to dictate the required effort levels during their roadwork or other cardio activity. So, for example, for the 20-minute run outlined above you would probably ask for:

- Easy walking: 1–2 minutes – RPE of around 8
- Power walking: 2 minutes – RPE 8–10
- Jogging: 5 minutes – RPE 10–12
- Fast striding: 5 x 30 seconds (1 minute recovery between each rep) – RPE of around 14 for the strides, and 6–8 for the recovery
- Easy jogging to finish – RPE 8–10
- Stretch

As well as breaking down a client's roadwork session into specific effort levels and recovery periods, why not suggest that they think and act like a boxer as they run? If they can get over any self-consciousness, it can be very effective to intersperse their running with a little shadow boxing, or even take their rope with them and skip as a warm-up or warm-down. Until they get the hang of this, you might take them out with you for a couple of 'boxing runs'. With those individuals who are new to running, you may in any case wish to supervise their first few sessions of roadwork, to make sure they understand how to pace and time their efforts correctly.

Finally, for every client, check that when they venture out alone they have a suitable method of timing themselves; are dressed visibly and appropriately for the weather and the workout; stretch well beforehand and afterwards; and are adequately hydrated. Ask them for feedback after their runs, and factor any positive progression or extra fatigue into their overall programme. You will find that even if they don't enjoy running as a general rule, it is gratifying to see the benefits to their overall fitness levels, as well as to their energy levels and performance during boxing sessions.

CIRCUIT TRAINING – THE 'BOXING CIRCUIT'

You will already know how to devise and teach a circuit, so there is no need to go into basics here. A great general conditioning tool, you can also tailor your client's circuit training to be boxing-specific – for example, by getting them to perform suitable exercises over effort periods that equate to boxing rounds, with the one-minute recovery times built in.

Below is just one tried-and-tested example of an effective 'boxing circuit': any of the exercises can be replaced with your own ideas. Bear in mind, too, that you can use the circuit as an alternative to another boxing fitness element – if the client has no access to a punch bag, or if they are training without your supervision, and thus can't do any focus pad work.

The circuit needs no equipment apart from a suitable timing device, and requires minimal space. When performed in full it takes up to an hour, but duration can easily be adapted according to clients' fitness levels and/or the time they have available (however, be sure never to reduce the recovery periods). Finally, this boxing circuit lends itself well to a class or group environment.

- Warm-up: pulse-raiser and stretch
- Shadow box (optional) – 3 x 3 minutes, 1 x minute's recovery between rounds (break these down for less experienced clients, see pages 75–8)
- Circuit: The following sequence is performed continuously three times, with no recovery. The whole effort should take three minutes, equivalent to one round:
  - 'Burpees' x 10
  - Star jumps x 10
  - Squat thrusts x 10
  - Split-leg squat thrusts x 10
  - Directional squat jumps x 10
  - Straight/tuck jumps 10
  - 1 x minute's rest

- The whole 'round' is then repeated as above, with 1 x minute's rest, and again a third and final time, finishing with 2 x minutes' rest
- Each of the same 6 exercises are then performed continuously over the course of 1 minute, with 1 x minute's recovery (i.e. 'burpees' x 1 minute, 1 x minute's rest, star jumps x 1 minute, 1 x minute's rest, and so on)
- Core exercises
- Warm-down

Depending on how fit they are, some clients may not be able to complete all the sets, especially over the minute-long efforts. Encourage them to keep going the best they can, getting into a rhythm and focusing their mind. If they are really struggling, it can help to give them a realistic goal to aim for: say they can manage 20 'burpees' over the course of a minute, they should aim to beat this by one rep each time they undertake the circuit. Over the course of a few months they will see their numbers building, which will boost their motivation.

As with every other training element in a boxing fitness programme, be inventive in setting your clients' circuit work. Try the 'ton up' circuit that is so popular with competitive boxers: this involves ten reps of ten different exercises (equalling one set), with 60 seconds between sets, and (ideally) ten sets. Each exercise is completed quickly, with a smooth transition to the next. Again, with less fit clients, reduce the number of sets, but to achieve the full training effect and keep the heart rate high, make sure they stick to the 10 x 10 format.

TAKING IT FURTHER

23

IF YOUR CLIENT WANTS TO SPAR OR COMPETE

You'll find that many, if not most, of your clients are happy working on their boxing fitness without ever wishing to take it further, into the realms of sparring and competition. As you will have gathered from the content of this book, the training routine is sufficiently flexible, progressive and challenging to keep them – and you – motivated and engaged in the long term. There is no need for any person-to-person contact in order to enjoy the range of physical and psychological benefits that boxing training confers.

However, there is no doubt that in recent years there has been wider public acknowledgement of improved safety standards in the competitive sport. In its amateur and professional forms, boxing today is strictly regulated by the respective governing bodies; trainers, managers, promoters and officials are now tasked first and foremost with the welfare and fair treatment of every participant.

This, combined with worldwide publicity surrounding ground-breaking performances by the boxers, both male and female, at London 2012, has made the sport a far more attractive proposition for competitive involvement – more

attractive to potential participants, as well as to schools, clubs and parents.

It is therefore entirely possible that as an exercise professional interested and involved in boxing, you will be approached by individuals who aspire to sparring and/or competition. And this ambition may not be restricted to young people: individuals who are over the age-limit (34 years) for an amateur or professional licence can still engage in competitive boxing, via the 'white collar' route mentioned on page 155. If you check out the website of the World White Collar Boxing Association (www.wwcba.org), you'll see from their figures that many thousands of people do indeed choose this route.

In order to make the right decision about what you can safely and legally offer such clients, you should first understand what is involved in both sparring and competition.

SPARRING

Sparring is the term applied to a short bout of 'practice competition' between two opponents. It is usually undertaken in a proper boxing ring, and always under qualified coaching supervision. Both parties must wear full protective equipment: head-guard, gumshield, groin protector, breast shields for females, and sparring gloves of an appropriate weight and quality.

Depending on the aim of the sparring session, it can involve full or restrained contact. *Technical* or *technique sparring* is undertaken with the intent to perfect a specific skill, rather than to re-create a competitive situation. In the run-up to a contest, for example, a boxer may study footage of his/her opponent and decide that they are vulnerable to body shots. Sparring sessions would then focus on 'working to the body' from different positions,

levels and angles, to maximise the boxer's advantage in the forthcoming bout.

Conditional or *condition sparring* is when two participants agree – or the trainer dictates – before the session commences, what is going to happen. For example, it may be determined that one boxer only is to throw punches, while the other rehearses their defence. And in *open sparring*, opponents box as if they were in a competitive situation, obviously maintaining their discipline and control at all times.

Technical and condition sparring in particular are great learning tools, not least because working in a 'live' situation with another boxer introduces an element of unpredictability – one which cannot be replicated by, for example, the punch bag or focus pads. Open sparring can give a good sense of how a contest will feel, as the boxer tests their body and reactions to the competitive experience. It should however be used sparingly, and only by relatively experienced boxers: the pressure of the situation affords little chance to learn and perfect new skills, and the likelihood of injury is increased.

While in theory there is nothing to stop you supervising light sparring sessions between two clients – provided that you all adhere to the safety rules detailed above – you must first ensure that your public liability insurance would provide cover in the eventuality of an incident or injury. You may feel perfectly able to control a bout of sparring, but unforeseen things do occur, and you'd be surprised at how quickly tempers can flare along with the adrenaline.

Do not allow yourself to be pushed into a situation that is beyond your or your client's ability and competence. It's just not necessary, and can result in misfortune. If you do make the considered decision to go ahead with this type of work, it is preferable by far to obtain a formal coaching qualification that will give you the knowledge and experience to confidently handle sparring sessions. To go about this, your first move should be to enquire at the local branch of your national sports governing body (see the 'Futher resources' section). Explain to them what you wish to do, and they will advise you.

If you are in the UK, and you have taken or are taking a course under the GB National Boxing Awards (www.boxingawards.co.uk/index.php, see also page 10), remember that the first three levels (Preliminary, Standard and Bronze) do *not* qualify you to teach contact boxing. Only the Silver, Gold and Platinum standards involve technique development via semi-contact or full-contact sparring.

An alternative to doing it yourself is to approach a local boxing club or gym and talk to one of the qualified coaches there. For a small fee, or even for the sake of helping out a fellow professional, they may agree to supervise a spar-

Note carefully that the section in this *Complete Guide* that addresses the necessary legislative and professional requirements of the instructor or trainer wishing to teach boxing *does not cover you for contact boxing*. Because of the added risk, sparring bouts should be supervised by an appropriately qualified person, to ensure a safe and controlled environment. Sparring should take place in a proper boxing ring, and full personal protective equipment must be worn by both participants: this means headguard, gumshield, groin protector, breast shields for women, and sparring gloves of the correct weight and quality.

ring session with your client on your behalf. They may even be able to provide a sparring partner who is of an equivalent weight, but of slightly superior ability and experience. Working with them will give your client a great deal of confidence, and you will be happy to secure a safe and controlled environment for them in which they can spread their wings.

COMPETITION

If your client would like to compete in the sport of boxing, they have three potential avenues in which to do so: amateur boxing; professional boxing; or white collar boxing. You should not consider taking on someone who is serious about a career in boxing without first possessing at least the minimum relevant coaching qualification. Again, consult the sport's governing body to find out where to start with this.

Here are a few facts about each of the three options, to give you an idea of which might be best suited to the client. Once you have discussed this together, and decided on an option, consider approaching a local club with a good reputation and talking to the coaches there. They might have the capacity to train your client while you are getting your qualification – and there is nothing to stop you continuing with the client's general fitness training in the meantime.

AMATEUR BOXING

As the name suggests, amateur boxers do not compete for financial gain: the ultimate prize is an Olympic gold medal. The sport is conducted in clubs, schools and universities/colleges, at the Olympics (since 1920) and Commonwealth Games (since 1930), and in other venues as sanctioned by the various arms of the sport's governing body – the International Boxing Association (AIBA). The AIBA website, www.aiba.org, provides news, events information, and documentation pertaining to the sport of amateur boxing, as well as contact details for, and links to, national federations and regional/local subdivisions.

The minimum age for competitive amateur boxing is 11 years, and the maximum, 34 years. To be eligible to compete, all boxers must have a full medical; if they are pronounced fit, then they are given official clearance (known as being 'carded').

Like professional boxers (see below), amateurs compete in weight divisions to ensure their safety and welfare – since, generally speaking, the heavier the individual, the more powerful the punch. For men, the lightest division is the 'light flyweight', at 48kg; the heaviest is the 'super heavyweight', where boxers weigh in at more than 91kg. (At present women, who competed at the Olympics for the first time in 2012, box in one of only three weight categories, but this is likely to change

soon.) As a further safety measure, below the age of 17 (when they are known as Juniors) amateur boxers cannot concede more than 12 months in age to their opponent.

Unlike professional boxers, who compete bare-chested and with no protective headgear, amateur boxers wear blue or red vests or singlets (to demonstrate which 'corner' they belong in); headguards are mandatory. Their gloves weigh 10 ounces. Scoring is by 'points': for a boxer to score a point, they must hit the opponent's head or body on a legally defined target area, making forceful contact with the knuckled part of the glove. Judges sit ringside, and record the points, either via a computerised scoring system, or with hand-held 'counters'.

There are no draws in amateur boxing. The winner of a bout is the boxer with the most points (so each boxer wins or loses 'on points'), unless the referee stops the bout before the final bell because one of the contestants is unable to continue – in which case the opponent is automatically the

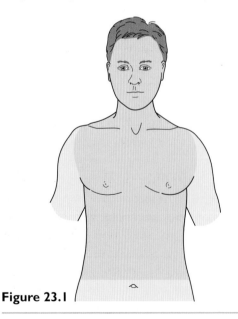

Figure 23.1

In both amateur and professional boxing, any punch delivered to an opponent's *body* – as opposed to the head – must be kept 'above the belt' to be legal. The belt is defined as an imaginary line which runs across the opponent's mid-section from hip-bones to navel: the attacker's glove must land above this line: 'above the belt'. The rules oblige all boxers (male, female, amateur and professional) to wear groin protection against stray 'low' shots. Strict warnings will be given for low blows, and persistent offenders may well be disqualified from the contest. Figure 23.1 shows the legal target area (shaded) for both head and body.

winner. If points arer equal at the end of a bout, a judge will determine the winner based on elements such as superior style or defence. Rounds may be between 1.5 and 3 minutes long, with three or four rounds generally comprising an amateur contest.

PROFESSIONAL BOXING

Professional boxers compete for a fee, known as a 'purse', which is shared with their trainer and manager. In championships, they box for a 'title' in their weight division: for example, they may be European and/or World Champion in the Light Welterweight Division. The title is accompanied by a trophy comprising an elaborately ornate belt, which has to be defended by or won from the boxer – together with their coveted title.

Professional bouts are longer than amateur bouts, typically ranging from 10 to 12 three-minute rounds. If the fight 'goes the distance' – in other words, is not stopped before the end – the winner will be chosen based on how many rounds the judges think a boxer has won. The referee can stop the bout at any time if he or she believes that one participant is unable to defend themselves; this is known as a 'technical knockout' (TKO). A TKO may also be awarded against a boxer if they simply stop boxing, or if their 'corner' stops the contest by literally 'throwing in the towel'. A 'knockout' occurs when a boxer simply cannot rise from the canvas, sufficiently recovered from the blow that felled them, to satisfy the referee that it is safe for them to continue.

Because injury is much more likely in professional than in amateur boxing, the licensing process is more demanding. To be eligible to box professionally, an individual must first sign a contract with a professional boxing trainer and manager, who will endorse their application to the relevant Board of Boxing Control. The boxer will then be interviewed and, if the Board is satisfied, it may make an appointment to watch them spar. If the sparring session is then approved, a stringent (and expensive) medical test follows, which includes a sight test and an MRI scan.

WHITE COLLAR BOXING

In the 1990s, a new phenomenon grew up in the US after the famous New York boxing gym, Gleason's, staged a contest between two Wall Street businessmen with no prior combat background. These City types had bet on which one of them would remain standing after three rounds in the ring, employing trainers and working out for six months before the showdown at Gleason's in front of a huge crowd of colleagues and friends. Thus 'white collar boxing' was born, since becoming widely popular. The websites www.wwcba.org and www.whitecollarboxingeurope.com list details of participating venues and organisations.

White collar boxing is open to both men and women aged between 25 and 57 years. Boxers compete in weight categories, with a 2.5kg 'tolerance' or legal weight differential in competition. Bouts are contested over three rounds of two minutes, with one-minute recovery intervals, and gloves are 16oz in weight. Headgear is mandatory, and groin protection compulsory for men and optional for women.

The scoring system is similar to that in professional boxing: each judge decides who wins each round, giving ten points to the winner and nine to the loser (or eight, if the winner dominated, or if the losing boxer also has a point deducted for a foul after the relevant warnings). The referee can stop the bout at any stage if, in their opinion, the safety of either participant is in question.

SAMPLE TRAINING SESSIONS

As has been the message conveyed throughout this book, one of the most enjoyable aspects of boxing fitness – from the point of view of the exercise professional – is that you can really make it your own. Once you and your clients have mastered the basic boxing techniques and are able to perform these safely and reasonably well, you can adapt the workout to suit everyone. From individual drills to sessions to whole programmes, bring your imagination to bear and have fun, while tailoring the work to individual or group requirements and achieving specific positive fitness gains.

This said, if boxing fitness is a relatively new tool in your professional armoury, it might be helpful to have some guidance in how to structure a session, as well as how and when to develop a workout to address the 'next level'. Of course the speed and ease with which a client will step up their workout depends upon each individual; not just on their physical abilities, but also on any constraints they may face while attempting to build an exercise programme into their busy lives. But you already possess the skill and judgement to consult, monitor and evaluate each person, and to adapt the work demands accordingly.

The following three sessions are offered simply as examples of how you might put together a single session: 1) for someone just starting out; 2) for someone at an intermediate level; and 3) for a client who is more advanced. The advanced session prescribed below is the kind of workout a competitive boxer might undertake, minus the sparring, so bear in mind that it is very hard work. In fact it is sound advice always to personally attempt each session you devise, before asking your student to do it. If you struggle, they are bound to.

As a very broad rule, to take a person from novice to advanced level (from Session 1 to Session 3) may well take a year or more of regular, progressive training, and it almost goes without saying that some clients will take much longer that that, while others will be super-fast. Be flexible, and most importantly, never let the workout be dull. If any of your exercises or sessions appear to be growing old, throw in a (figurative) curve-ball that will continue to challenge and excite.

Finally, consider this: while most people will really take to boxing fitness, and thoroughly enjoy developing increasingly advanced skills, others may not. There is no onus on you or on them to progress beyond the basics, which are in any case effective when properly employed. More advanced boxing techniques require a lot of physical and mental manoeuvring, and there are those who, through no-one's fault, just won't get the hang of it – just as some individuals take to driving a car almost as second nature, while a few will cut you up no matter how many years they have under their seatbelt. That's OK. If you encounter such a client, structure their training programme around what they enjoy best and, if there's room within it, cherry-pick the boxing elements they *can* do, and incorporating them with flair.

Boxing Fitness Session: Level – Beginner/Novice

(Duration: I hour approx.) Minutes (mins)/Rounds (rnds)

Note: During this session you will judge how quickly to progress as you watch how the client copes with the training. Build on the basics by (i) introducing more complex techniques and combinations, bringing in footwork and defences as appropriate, (ii) adding rounds, (iii) increasing the intensity of the work. Never make the sessions harder by reducing recovery periods. Depending on how often you train with the client, it may take 3–6 months for a novice to move to the intermediate level.

Mins/Rnds (recovery period)	Activity (equipment needed) and page ref	Comments
3–5 mins	Wrap your client's hands (hand-wraps) see pages 24–7	The first time you do this, spend a little extra time demonstrating the technique and allowing the client to practise. They will soon learn to wrap their own hands, and may even arrive at the session already prepared. Make sure they understand the importance of protecting the small bones in their hands and wrists from injury, especially in the early days when they are learning the shots and combinations.
10–15 mins	Warm-up: pulse-raiser; stretches (dynamic and/or static); final pulse-raiser see pages 23–4	To avoid the generic warm-up and make it more boxing specific, use your imagination: for example, for the pulse-raiser, get them jogging around the venue, punching up in the air, out in front, rolling their arms and so on. Ensure that stretches cover the full range of joints and muscles, not just the upper body. Your clients should be completely warmed-up before beginning any kind of boxing techniques.
10–15 mins	Introduce/practise stance, guard, straight shots and combinations see pages 30–6	With the beginner/novice client, you will need to spend a good part of each session introducing and recapping on the basic boxing techniques, including stance and guard. At the beginning, this will take some time; be alert to their boredom threshold and don't try to introduce too much too quickly. As they progress through their programme, all they will need is a quick reminder before you move into some shadow boxing. Stick to the straight shots (jab, cross/back hand) and combinations until you really feel they are ready to move on to hooks and uppercuts.
2 rnds of 2 mins (I min between rnds)	Shadow boxing (hands wrapped; mirror) see pages 75–8	Bring in the concept of the boxing 'round', and get them used to the feel of it by leading some shadow boxing. If there is a mirror in the venue, show them how they can use their own reflection to 'box' against. Pitch the shadow boxing at their level: in other words, don't introduce complex footwork if you haven't already covered it in a teaching session. And encourage them to keep going through the full round, even if they need to stop every now and then, 'shake it out' and take a breather – always whilst keeping their hands up.

SAMPLE TRAINING SESSIONS

2 rnds of 2 mins (1 min between rnds)	Punch bag/focus pads (*client: hands wrapped beneath sparring gloves; instructor: use punch bag or focus pads*) see pages 62–4 and 86–91	Then give them something to hit! Depending on the equipment available at the venue, this can be the punch bag and/or the focus pads. If you are using both, do a couple of rounds on the punch bag, then introduce skipping (see below), and follow up with some basic focus pad work. Stay with straight shots and combinations, and simple footwork. At this early stage in their programme, the client is likely to find the punching work very tiring, so give them loads of encouragement – make it interactive. Above all, don't let them give up: it's important that they understand the importance of completing a round, even if that round is broken up into more management periods of effort and 'breathers'. Stick rigidly to the one-minute recovery period at all times.
2 rnds of 2 mins (1 min between rnds)	Skipping (*hands wrapped; speed rope*) see pages 81–5	This is likely to be the most frustrating technique for your client to master. After explaining and demonstrating the technique(s), all you can really do is watch, praise and encourage them. Focus on the positives; on their progress during each session, and from session to session too. Tell them everyone finds skipping really difficult at first. As with all other boxing work, keep them going through the full round, judging carefully when they need to stop and take a breather before continuing until it is time for their minute's recovery.
10 mins	Core exercises (*mat; Swiss ball*) see pages 144–6	Take off their hand-wraps and give your client a good drink and towel down before progressing on to some core work. In the first instance, make sure they understand what the core is, and the importance – both to functional fitness and to sporting performance – of good core strength and stability. Make the exercises as fun as possible, and bear in mind that novices will (should) have found these early boxing fitness sessions hard work. Sit-ups done after unfamiliar punching will hurt – a lot. Go easy until you feel they are ready to step it up.
5 mins	Warm down see pages 23–7	Stretch with your client, and take this opportunity to talk to them about DOMS – the muscle stiffness they will encounter in the days following these early sessions. A thorough warm down will help reduce this, so don't let them rush off. Remind them to keep well hydrated after their workout, and summarise their progress so they leave feeling energised and confident.

Boxing Fitness Session: Level – Intermediate

(Duration: 1 hour 10 mins approx.) Minutes (mins)/Rounds (rnds)

Note: You can build on this session by adding rounds and increasing intensity (speed, power, etc.). By now you will have introduced the hooks and uppercuts. Note that rounds have increased from 2 to the full 3 minutes – they should never be longer than this. Increase frequency by adding rounds, rather than duration. Always maintain the 1-minute recovery between rounds. It may take 3-6 months for an intermediate to move to the advanced level.

Mins/Rnds (recovery period)	Activity (equipment needed) and page ref	Comments
2 mins	Wrap your client's hands – or they wrap their own (hand-wraps) see pages 24–7	This technique should now be second nature. The client may well wrap their own hands, but it can be a nice touch for the instructor to do it quickly and efficiently, having a brief chat about how things are going and the nature of the session to follow. You can use this as an opportunity to judge your client's state of mind and body – and adjust your session plan if necessary.
5-10 mins	Warm-up: pulse-raisers and stretches (dynamic and/or static) see pages 23–4	As long as you cover the requisite pulse-raisers and stretches, you can make the generic warm-up a little shorter at the intermediate level – since clients will progress straight on to several rounds of energetic shadow boxing. Consider how you might incorporate ways of recapping on the basic boxing techniques as part of the warm-up. Alternatively, follow the warm-up with a brief reminder of the key teaching points: stance, guard, shots and combinations, footwork, defence.
3 rnds of 3 mins (1 min between rnds)	Shadow boxing (hands wrapped; mirror) see pages 75–8	By now your client will be sufficiently confident to undertake 3 good rounds of active shadow boxing, keeping going for the duration of each round. You should watch and/or lead, engaging constantly with what they are doing and calling out some teaching tips or corrections and balancing these with praise and encouragement. Remember, although shadow boxing is a great opportunity for boxers to practise their techniques, the main aim here is to improve your client's fitness and get them to have fun, so don't keep pulling them up if they make minor errors. It can be a good idea to give your student a rough guide about what you're looking for in each round. As just one example, try: • Round 1: using only straight shots and combinations • Round 2: introducing hooks and uppercuts, singly and in combination • Round 3: practising the various shots and combinations with footwork and some defensive moves If you have access to a boxing ring, get them to shadow box there – it's great for motivation and will inspire them to try different ways of moving around the canvas. Or use a mirror, asking them to view themselves as their 'shadow opponent' and watching them from the side, behind and at different angles to see where they may be struggling. Between rounds, give them a sip of water and towel off any sweat.

3 rnds of 3 mins (1 min between rnds)	Punch bag – if available (client: hands wrapped beneath sparring gloves; instructor: use of punch bag) see pages 62–4	**Note:** *If there is no punch bag at your venue, omit this stage and move on to skipping (see below). When focus pads are your only opportunity to practise contact punching with a client, it's best to keep this until the end of the session, just before the core work and the warm down. It's the most fun part of any boxing fitness session – save it till the grunt work is done, and really enjoy!* As with the shadow boxing, above, engage actively in your client's punch bag work, holding on to the bag at times and calling out guidance about the kind of shots and combinations you'd like them to do. Allow them time to step back off the bag, shake out their arms and take a breather before returning to the guard and moving in to resume punching. This is hard effort and they will need to be pushed and encouraged to complete each 3-minute round. Watch out for signs of knuckle soreness and stop the bag work if this seems to be worsening. Their hands will gradually toughen up as the programme progresses.
3 rnds of 3 mins (1 min between rnds)	Skipping (hands wrapped; speed rope) see pages 81–5	Even at the intermediate level, skipping may prove a frustrating skill for your client. Recap on the basic technique(s), and then simply watch, praise and encourage them as they work through the rounds. When they falter and stumble, which they will – even the most seasoned boxers do – let them know that this is OK, and get them to start again. And again. *Don't* be tempted to turn away while the student skips; you risk allowing them to feel abandoned and negative about their progress. Instead, focus on the positives, and when they master the basics, introduce more complex techniques, which will motivate them to keep on trying to improve.
2 rnds of 3 mins (1 min between rnds)	Focus pads (client: hands wrapped beneath sparring gloves; instructor: focus pads) see pages 86–91	The best bit for both of you – really have fun with it. Start with the straight shots and combinations, and gradually build in more complex punching, with and without footwork and defence. Introduce a range of drills according to what fitness element(s) you are focusing on. If you have had to omit the punch bag element from your session, do more on the focus pads, but remember that it will be extremely tiring for the client: pace them, and yourself. The best focus pad work will leave them panting for breath and completely spent, but already looking forward to more …
5-10 mins	Core exercises (mat; Swiss ball) see pages 144–6	After the focus pad work, take off their hand-wraps and give your client a good drink and towel down before progressing on to some core work. At this stage, you may already be building core strength and stability into your chosen focus pad drills – so adjust this part of the session accordingly.
5 mins	Warm down see pages 23–7	Stretch with your client, discuss the session, and give them plenty of praise as you review the progress they are making with their boxing fitness. Make sure they leave feeling happy and positive. Remind them to stay well hydrated between sessions, and to eat and sleep well; this will aid in their recovery and give them optimum strength and energy for their boxing programme.

Boxing Fitness Session: Level – Advanced

(Duration: 1 hour 30 mins approx.) Minutes (mins)/Rounds (rnds)

Note: If you started work with this client when a novice, you would expect to have trained them regularly and frequently for at least a year before reaching this kind of level. Rounds are all 3 minutes, with a minute's recovery; for punch bag and focus pad work, they may prefer to wear lighter bag gloves rather than sparring gloves. All the boxing techniques are involved, and obviously, it is your choice as to how many rounds to set for each discipline – below is simply one example. Work on speed, power and co-ordination; build by adding rounds for each discipline, or increasing intensity during rounds. An advanced client may well need to train between your sessions – perhaps doing some solo roadwork and/or circuits. At this level, boxing fitness is extremely intensive: keep an eye on your clients' diet, hydration levels and rest/recovery.

Mins/ Rnds) (recovery period)	Activity (equipment needed) and page ref	Comments
5-10 mins	Warm-up: pulse-raisers and stretches (dynamic and/or static) see pages 23-4	At this level the client should be quite familiar with warm-up principles and practice, and be able to proceed with minimal input from you. Don't let them get lazy, though: these advanced boxing sessions are intensive, and require thorough preparation.
3 rnds of 3 mins (1 min between rnds)	Shadow boxing (hands wrapped) see pages 75–8	You are looking for clean, fluid work which addresses all the shots and combinations with balanced footwork, counterpunching and defensive movements. Watch too for psychological elements such as focus and discipline. At this level the shadow boxing serves as a warm-up, a chance to practise techniques, and a preparation for the hard work of the session to come.
5 rnds of 3 mins (1 min between rnds)	Punch bag – if available (client: hands wrapped beneath sparring/bag gloves; instructor: use of punch bag) see pages 62–4	They should work hard throughout each round, with a good range of strong shots and combinations and little rest beyond the minute between rounds. Watch for a dropped guard and for the finer technical points such as hip and shoulder pivot into the shots. Work on power, speed and endurance, as well as focus and discipline in their approach. As your clients progress at this level, you yourself will be challenged to think up ways of keeping them motivated and engaged in their punch bag work, which is hard and can feel lonely. Be actively engaged in their training – hold the bag, shout and yell a bit, give lots of feedback and praise. Towel them off every now and then and give them some water. Between rounds, encourage deep diaphragmatic breathing for the full minute's recovery period.

Boxing Fitness Session: Level – Advanced (*cont.*)

3 rnds of 3 mins (*1 min between rnds*)	Skipping (*hands wrapped; speed rope*) see pages 81–5	Skipping should be much easier for your clients at this stage in their programme. At the very least they should be skipping steadily for an entire round without needing to stop and rest; they may well be trying more than one technique. Encourage them to 'mix it up' – for example, they might spend one round alternating 30 seconds' really fast work with 30 seconds' slow and steady skipping; or they might change from technique to technique (high knees, running with the rope, cross-overs, double-unders) every 30 seconds. Try not to let them coast too much if they find skipping quite easy – they should still undertake the work to the best of their ability, as it will boost their cardio fitness as well as teaching them to focus on co-ordination and deft footwork.
3 rnds of 3 mins (*1 min between rnds*)	Focus pads (*client: hands wrapped beneath sparring/bag gloves; instructor: focus pads*) see pages 86–91	You will find it tricky to take an advanced client on the focus pads effectively if you haven't mastered the pads to a similar level – so it's important that you continue your own practice and work on your own techniques in order to make the grade. If they are very strong and fast and you are a little unsure, stick to the straight shots and combinations, but make them work as hard as possible during the rounds: a good tip is to include plenty of footwork and other supplementary movements (e.g. incorporate squats, or circuit exercises between punching) to keep them busy and their heart rate raised. Making them punch whilst moving backwards will really tax them, as will getting them to punch at high speed and with less input or 'feed' from the pads. It's unusual to find someone who is so fit that you can't make them suffer … which, as has been stated many times in this book, is one of the beauties of boxing fitness training!
10-15 mins	Core exercises, circuit training, cardio work (*various*) see pages 144–6	At a really high level, you may wish to continue working your client after the focus pad element of their session, by setting some core work and/or introducing some resistance training, circuit exercises or additional cardio activity – depending on what equipment is available at your venue. It is your job to judge how hard to push an individual, and to adapt the session requirements to their current fitness level and abilities. Don't stress them so hard that they feel demotivated and exhausted – but don't let them leave feeling that they haven't really stretched themselves either. Finding this balance is a skill in itself, which will come with practice and experience as you train a range of people with widely differing needs.
5 mins	Warm down see pages 23–7	As always, stretch with your client, discuss the session, and give them plenty of praise as you review the progress they are making with their boxing fitness. Make sure they leave feeling happy and positive.

RESOURCES

BOXING EQUIPMENT

For yourself, or for recommending to your clients, boxing clothing and equipment is now available from a wide range of online stockists. The following is a small selection of tried-and-tested suppliers, but feel free to research your own. If you are located outside the UK, all these sites will ship internationally:

- www.titleboxing.com
- www.ringside.com
- www.lemarr.com
- www.boxfituk.com
- www.sugarrays.co.uk
- www.yorkfitness.com/shop/Boxing
- www.lonsdale.com
- www.sportsdirect.com/boxing
- www.pugsports.co.uk

At the time of writing, Everlast – an iconic boxing brand – will only ship within the US from its dedicated website, www.everlast.com. However, Everlast clothing and equipment can be ordered via Amazon and other large online stores, or even in your high street sports shops.

Many elite boxers have now created their own branded merchandise, which is available via their websites. Among these, try:

- www.shop.hattonboxing.com (Ricky Hatton, former World Champion, Light Welterweight division)
- www.goldenboystore.com (Oscar De La Hoya, ten times World Champion in six weight divisions)
- www.hayemaker.com (David Haye, former WBA World Heavyweight Champion)
- www.floydmayweather.com (Floyd Mayweather, five-division World Champion)
- www.amirkhanworld.com (Amir Khan, four-time World Champion)
- www.klitschko.com (the Klitschko brothers – between them, holding every world title in the Heavyweight division, with the exception of the WBA)

Adidas now manufactures some excellent boxing gear, which you can explore via the links at www.adidas.com. And for the crème-de-la-crème of boxing equipment, dream about owning some focus pads by Cleto Reyes, www.cletoreyes.com.

BOXING FITNESS AND COACHING CERTIFICATION

There are a large number of international, national, regional and local organisations that offer routes to professional certification in both contact and non-contact boxing training. It's difficult to recommend any particular company or course, or even to list them, because – unless the training is done online – they are usually country- and/or venue-specific. Here are two examples.

Punchfit (www.punchfit.com.au), an Australian company, runs country-wide courses focusing on the trainer's technique in both boxing and pad work. They are accredited through Fitness Australia and Physical Activity Australia, and offer CPD points when successfully completed.

In the UK, PadBox (www.padbox.co.uk) runs focus pad courses that have been researched and designed by established amateur boxers and sports scientists. Different levels of qualification are available, and on successful completion candidates receive certification, a training manual and a DVD. PadBox is accredited by Skills Active and carries the maximum CPD points.

To find the course you're looking for, try doing your own, targeted research on the internet. If you can obtain a personal recommendation from friends or colleagues, this is invaluable, because the last thing you want is to spend time and money on an inferior product. Try to make sure that any course you choose is accredited by a recognised fitness industry body, and preferably carries some CPD points.

If you already have a PT qualification, you might approach your original training provider – for example, in the UK, the YMCA (www.ymcafit.org.uk) or Premier Training International (www.premierglobal.co.uk) – and ask their advice in how to specialise in boxing training. Organisations such as the Register of Exercise Professionals (REPs, www.exerciseregister.org), which has an international confederation, hold databases of CPD and Training courses, with boxing featuring among them – check out their course search facility online.

Earlier in the book (see pages 10 and 53) we discussed the GB National Boxing Awards (www.boxingawards.co.uk), which offer coaching courses in amateur boxing at six different levels. For your country/region, refer to the appropriate arm of the sport's governing body to enquire about any equivalent offer. Staff will give you guidance as to what certification you can obtain under their auspices, and how to go about it; contact details may be found by following the links under 'Governing bodies' below. Details are also given for the regulatory bodies for professional and white collar boxing.

Finally, don't forget the ABA's new REPs accredited training proghramme for the fitness market – 'BOX'. Find out more at www.abae.co.uk under 'Boxing for Fitness' – just follow the links.

GOVERNING BODIES
AMATEUR BOXING

- **www.aiba.org** The International Boxing Association, originally the Association Internationale de Boxe Amateur and still referred to as the AIBA. Sanctions amateur boxing matches, and awards world and subordinate championships.

- **www.usaboxing.org** The official website of USA Boxing – the national governing body for amateur boxing in the States.

- **www.eubcboxing.org** The European governing body for amateur boxing. The site includes tournament dates, online newsletter, rules, history, links to all committees and contact information.

- **www.abae.co.uk** The Amateur Boxing Association (ABA). As a national governing body, the ABA is responsible for administering, developing and promoting amateur boxing throughout England.

- **www.goldengloves.com** This programme leads the way in promoting amateur boxing in the States, and produces many competitors for America's boxing teams in the Pan-Am and Olympic Games.

PROFESSIONAL BOXING

Note: Professional boxing has a number of governing bodies, each sanctioning different contests and awarding different championship titles. This can be confusing, as it may lead to the existence of multiple world champions in any weight division. Below are the three main organisations: websites include brief histories, boxer rankings, schedules, results, a list of current champions, federation by-laws, and rules and regulations.

- **www.wbaonline.com** The World Boxing Association (WBA) – professional boxing's oldest governing body, founded in 1921.
- **www.wbcboxing.com** The World Boxing Council (WBC), established in 1963.
- **www.ibf-usba-boxing.com** The International Boxing Federation (IBF).

In Great Britain, the governing body for professional boxing is the British Boxing Board of Control (BBBofC), www.bbbofc.com. For the rest of Europe, visit www.boxebu.com and follow the links.

In America no single, unified governing body exists; individual state-controlled commissions have different sets of standards, rules and guidelines. For a list of the commissions and links, go to www.ringsidebygus.com.

WHITE COLLAR BOXING

The umbrella governing body is the World White Collar Boxing Association, and the website www.wwcba.org gives information and membership details for competitors, training establishments, trainers/coaches, events and promotions, and officials.

ONLINE RESOURCES

Inevitably, you will find yourself doing a lot of internet browsing in order to identify sources of reliable boxing training advice. It's important to be discerning: much of the information out there – especially with regard to focus pad work – pertains to mixed martial arts, whose practitioners do things differently (not least using feet, knees and elbows in ways which really, really shouldn't feature in your boxing fitness sessions!).

YouTube does feature some excellent videos, if you are selective. Try to narrow your search criteria as carefully as possible, to include such phrases as 'technical boxing training skills and drills' or 'focus pad training for boxers'. If you use the resource in conjunction with the advice given in this book, you should be able to find some good complementary guidance, both for your own boxing techniques and to pass on to your clients.

The following is a short list of useful sites, with a brief description. Bear in mind that, as with all things on the internet, they may be subject to change, with new ones taking their place.

www.bbc.co.uk

At this link http://news.bbc.co.uk/sport1/hi/boxing/get_involved/4253708.stm you can find the BBC's 'Get involved' guide to the basics of boxing. This gives excellent, simple advice on the skills and techniques, with further links.

www.boxing.isport.com

Still incomplete at the time of going to press, this looks set to be a good international resource – featuring boxing and training guides, videos, and help with 'connecting' with others in your location.

www.expertboxing.com

The basics of boxing for all beginners. Features information on punching, stance, footwork, training, sparring and how to find a good boxing gym.

www.gbboxing.org.uk

Search for GB Boxing Masterclass (video) on this site, where a national coach and successful young amateur demonstrate the boxing basics in a series of clear training clips.

www.myboxingcoach.com

A great online resource that isolates the individual boxing skills, and demonstrates them in videos and associated articles. Lots of content is free to non-members, and there is an eBook also available on subscription. As well as more than 40 free skills videos, the site features advice on equipment, training and coaching, nutrition, boxing psychology and fight analysis.

www.padbox.co.uk

In addition to advertising its focus pad courses for personal trainers and other exercise professionals, this site has some brief videos to show different levels of expertise with the mitts, together with a range of shots and combinations. PadBox was founded by a former amateur boxer turned professional boxing trainer.

www.rossboxing.com

Although this site bills itself as 'Real training advice for real fighters' – which sounds pretty macho – and is a little confusing to navigate, it contains lots of good information, articles and videos for the exercise professional. Take some time to explore it, and check out the blog at the link, www.rosstraining.com.

www.sugarboxing.com

Boxing, but with fewer words and more illustrations (very effective animated gifs). Different articles on technique, drills, strategy and conditioning.

A NOTE ON PRINTED RESOURCES

There are plenty of good books out there which describe and illustrate the fitness boxing workout. As well as *Boxing Fitness* by Clinton McKenzie and Hilary Lissenden (Bloomsbury Sport, 2011), Ian Oliver's *Boxing Fitness: A Guide to Get Fighting Fit* is ever-popular and available in paperback and as a DVD.

Another UK author, Gary Blower, published *Boxing: Training, Skills and Techniques* (Crowood Press) in 2007, and in 2011 Crowood Press brought out *Advanced Boxing: Training, Skills and Techniques* by Rakesh Sondhi and Tommy Thompson.

Outside the UK, in 2012 Dominique Paris published *A Fitness and Boxing Training Camp: Get in Fighting Shape* (Kindle edition; Knockout Coaching LLC, 2012), and Mark Hatmaker the *Boxer's Book of Conditioning and Drilling* (Tracks Publishing, 2012); his *Boxing Mastery*, co-authored by Doug Werner, was published in 2004.

Werner has also written *Boxer's Start-Up: A Beginner's Guide to Boxing* (1998) and, with Alan Lachica in 2000, *Fighting Fit: Boxing Workouts, Techniques, and Sparring*. Another title worth a mention is Ross O'Donnell's *The Ultimate Fitness Boxing & Kickboxing Workout* (Trafford Press, 2005).

Additionally you could refer to Andy and Jamie Dumas' *Knockout Fitness* (Skyhorse Publishing, 2009); *The Gleason's Gym Total Body Boxing*

Workout for Women (Simon & Schuster, August 2006); Cappy Kotz, *Boxing for Everyone – How to Get Fit and Have Fun With Boxing* (Amanda Lore, 1998); Danna Scott, *Boxing – The Complete Guide to Training and Fitness* (Pedigree Books, 2000); and Tom Seabourne, *Complete Idiot's Guide to Fitness Boxing Illustrated* (Alpha Books, 2006).

While these books may to a greater or lesser degree give you a thorough grounding in the principles and practice of boxing training, they are aimed primarily at practitioners rather than coaches. This is not to say that you won't find their content useful, having some practical application for you as you develop your clients' boxing fitness programme. But at present, comprehensive resources for the boxing fitness trainer, in hard copy form at least, are hard to find.

Browse the above publications, and look at rapidly expanding online resources that are available to you; a few of these are listed above. In addition, you will want to consult the following titles:

Know the Game: Boxing

by Kevin Hickey (Bloomsbury Sport, 2006)
A no-nonsense introduction to the sport of boxing – for you and for your client. All the basics, including equipment, rules, techniques and training tips. Written and endorsed by the sport's professional body.

The Complete Guide to Sports Nutrition

by Anita Bean (Bloomsbury Sport, new edition 2013)
The definitive practical handbook on nutrition for training and sporting performance. Contains all you will need to know, and more, to help guide you in your own diet, as well as advising your clients on eating and drinking their way to a successful boxing fitness programme. It includes specific advice for women, children and vegetarians.

Other titles in this *Complete Guide* series, which is aimed specifically at the exercise professional, may provide helpful supplementary sources of information – such as Matt Lawrence's *The Complete Guide to Core Stability* (same publisher).

Amateur boxing: as opposed to *professional boxing* – they are two completely separate sports. Since 1941 amateur boxing has been regulated by the world governing body, the International Boxing Association (AIBA). Boxers wear either red or blue strips, protective headguards and gloves weighing 10 ounces. *Bouts* are decided by ringside judges, with the result based on the number of scoring punches that land on a legal 'target area'. Amateur boxing is practised in schools, colleges and clubs, at the Olympic and Commonwealth Games, and elsewhere as sanctioned by the relevant national or regional governing bodies. In London in 2012, history was made when amateur boxing for women first became a fully ratified Olympic event.

Back hand: see *cross*.

Bag gloves: a type of boxing glove worn for any type of punching that involves no contact with another person – for example, when hitting the *punch bag*, *speed ball* or *focus pads*. Bag gloves are lighter than *sparring gloves*. They have a free-moving rather than a stitched 'thumb', and are loose rather than bound or laced at the wrist/ lower arm.

Bent-arm shots: the *hook* and the *uppercut*, as opposed to the *straight shots* – the *jab* and the *cross/back hand*.

Bobbing and weaving: see *defence*.

Body shot: a punch delivered to an opponent's body, rather than their head. Body shots are legal as long as they land on the front or sides of the torso, in the target area above the waist or 'belt'.

Bout: another name for a boxing contest. Bouts vary in the number of *rounds* they last. Professional championship bouts are 12 rounds long; amateur bouts usually comprise 3 rounds. In amateur boxing, bouts should never be referred to as 'fights'.

Boxing clock: a special clock which indicates the passage of *rounds* and rest (recovery) periods, via a bell or other electronic signal.

Boxing fitness: a form of boxing-based workout which incorporates all the elements of a traditional boxer's training regime, but without any glove-to-person contact. Boxing fitness is sometimes confused with 'boxercise', an aerobics-based class usually done to music, and incorporating a range of combat-type activities for increased fitness gains. For a true understanding of boxing fitness, think 'old school boxing training', without the risk.

Boxing gloves: see *bag gloves* and *sparring gloves*.

Boxing ring: see *ring*.

Combinations: groups or sequences of punches ('punches in bunches'), as opposed to individual shots (see *jab, cross/back hand, hook, uppercut*).

Condition(al) sparring: see *sparring*.

Counterpunching (or countering): 'answering' an opponent's shots – punching back in direct response.

Cross: also known as the *back hand*. Like the jab, a *straight shot*, but this time delivered from the rear (back) hand across the boxer's body.

Cross-overs: an advanced skipping technique in which the arms are crossed at the elbows on the downward arc of the rope.

Defence: the collective term for a range of techniques employed by the boxer to avoid, block or ward off an opponent's attacking shots: for example, *ducking*, *slipping*, *bobbing and weaving*, and *push-aways* from a punch or combination.

Division: a term used for the weight categories within which boxers compete in order to ensure an equitable *bout*. For example, Britain's Nicola Adams competed in the London 2012 Olympic Games in the flyweight division, for female boxers weighing 51kg.

Ducking: see *defence*.

Focus pads: also called focus mitts or hook-and-jab pads, these comprise a glove into which a qualified trainer slips their fingers, usually secured at the wrist with a Velcro strip. The mitts are filled with aerated foam padding designed to absorb and disperse the impact of a boxer's punches, thus reducing strain on the trainer's joints. The trainer can hold the focus pads in different positions, and at different ranges and angles, so that the full range of punches and *combinations* can be rehearsed. Focus pad work is as close to 'real boxing' as your client can get, without any glove-to-person contact.

Footwork: simply, the way in which a boxer moves his or her body effectively to get in and out of range (see *reach*) of their opponent. In fact, good footwork is anything but simple, requiring excellent agility, balance, co-ordination and timing.

Groin protector: personal protective equipment worn by both amateur and professional boxers.

Guard: the way in which a boxer holds their arms and hands – the classic 'hands up' position, which literally guards the head against an opponent's attack.

Gumshield (mouth guard): worn to protect a boxer's mouth and teeth from damage caused by blows to the chin and jaw. Mandatory in both amateur and professional contests, these should also be worn by anyone undertaking *sparring*.

Hand-wraps: lengths of cotton or elastic-type material used to 'wrap' the hands before boxing gloves are donned for training or competition. Hand-wraps prevent the skin of the hands from chafing, and protect the small bones of the hands and wrists from potential injury. They are also worn for reasons of hygiene, since – unlike boxing gloves – they can be laundered.

Headguard: a type of padded 'helmet' worn for *sparring* and in all *amateur boxing* contests, designed to protect the boxer's head and face from damage inflicted by an opponent's punches. Professional boxers do not wear protective headgear.

Heavy bag: see *punch bag*.

Hook: one of the *bent-arm shots* (see also *uppercut*). The hook is a semi-circular punch, designed to make impact with the side of an opponent's head or chin, or with their torso.

Jab: a *straight shot*, always delivered with the lead (front) hand, straight out from the boxer's shoulder. The jab can be aimed at the head or body.

Open sparring: see *sparring*.

Orthodox: see *stance*.

Professional boxing: as opposed to *amateur boxing* – they are two completely separate sports.

Boxers compete for a fee, known as a 'purse'; they box bare-chested and wear no protective headguard. Bouts are scored by 'decision' made by a referee and/or judges sitting ringside.

Punch bag: sometimes referred to as the 'heavy bag'. A type of padded 'bag', often cylindrical in shape, used to provide a cushioned resistance to shots and *combinations* as the boxer trains to improve fitness and technique. There are a number of different punch bags available, of various sizes/weights/responsiveness – see also *speed ball*.

Push-away: see *defence*.

Queensberry Rules: introduced in 1867 under the patronage of the Marquess of Queensberry, these 12 rules regulated the ancient bare-knuckled sport of prize fighting and formed the basis of modern boxing. The rules established (among other controls) the use of a roped-off boxing *ring*, timed *rounds*, and padded gloves for the protection of both participants.

Reach: the range of a punch. If a boxer has relatively long arms, he or she is said to have the advantage of 'good natural reach'.

Ring: the boxing ring is actually a square, comprising a raised platform covered with padding and a durable canvas. There is a post at each corner, to which are fixed four parallel pairs of ropes. These form a flexible, continuous barrier that prevents boxers from falling off the platform when *sparring* or competing.

Roadwork: the boxer's traditional term for running.

Rounds: intervals of training or competitive effort. Professional boxers compete over three-minute rounds; in amateur boxing, rounds may be between one-and-a-half and three minutes long (two for women). The rest interval between every round, in both sports, is one minute.

Shadow boxing: literally, 'boxing at shadows'. The boxer practises their shots, *combinations*, *footwork*, *defence* and *counterpunching* as if there were an opponent in front of them, when in fact they are alone.

Sideways (or side) on: see *square on*.

Slipping: see *defence*.

Sparring: the term used to describe practice *bouts* between two individuals under coaching supervision. Protective equipment is worn by both parties. Sparring may be referred to as *technique*, *condition(al)* or *open*, depending on the specific aim of the session. Technique sparring focuses on improving a particular skill. Condition(al) sparring is done under certain conditions, which are agreed beforehand – for example, one boxer throws only *straight shots*; the other only defends. Open sparring is unrestricted, preparing the boxers for the pressure and fitness demands of competition.

Sparring gloves: a type of boxing glove worn for any type of punching that involves contact with another person (see also *sparring*). Sparring gloves are more substantial and padded than *bag gloves*; they extend and fasten further up the wrist/lower arm, with the thumb stitched to the body of the glove.

Speed ball: a small, air-filled *punch bag* anchored to a 'rebound platform' that is mounted parallel to the ground. The ball is used to improve speed and hand-eye co-ordination.

Square on: standing 'square on' to an opponent, the boxer is positioned with their whole body facing forwards, so that the mid-section is exposed and thus vulnerable to *body shots*. In the correct *stance*, the mid-section is pivoted slightly '*sideways (or side) on*' – sometimes called 'bladed' – to the opponent, with the boxer's lower body turned towards the rear foot while keeping the front foot, hip and shoulders in line.

Stance: the way in which a boxer stands when punching. The stance may be with the left foot in front, known as 'orthodox', or with the right foot in front, known as 'southpaw'. See also *guard*.

Straight shots: the *jab* and the *cross*. The latter punch is known as the *back hand* in amateur boxing. *Bent-arm shots* are the *hook* and the *uppercut*.

Technique sparring: see *sparring*.

Uppercut: one of the *bent-arm shots*, a 'vertical' punch thrown up towards the target, which may be an opponent's head or body.

White collar boxing: a fully regulated form of the sport, open to men and women aged 25 to 57, allowing those who do not hold an amateur or professional licence to get into the ring in a competitive environment with added safety measures. Regulatory bodies are the International White Collar Boxing Association (IWCBA), and the World White Collar Boxing Association (WWCBA).

CLIENT/TRAINER AGREEMENT (SAMPLE)

- The trainer will use their skills and knowledge to design a safe programme of boxing fitness-based exercise that will take into account the personal goals, fitness levels and activity likes and dislikes of the client.
- The trainer will provide the coaching, supervision advice and support that the client may need to help them achieve their goals. The client's progress will be regularly monitored, and the boxing fitness programme revised and adjusted accordingly.
- The trainer will provide all necessary equipment, and will organise appropriate venues for all sessions.
- All client information will be kept strictly private and confidential. If the trainer requires further medical information from a practitioner, the client must provide such details.
- It is understood between client and trainer that both will commit to the programme and give 100% effort.
- The client is required to arrive 5 minutes prior to a training session so that a full session can be achieved on each visit.
- The client is required to wear appropriate clothing and footwear. Clothes should be loose fitting and non-restrictive. Footwear should be comfortable and provide adequate support.

TERMS AND CONDITIONS
HEALTH SCREENING

- All clients must complete a PAR-Q before commencing any exercise programme.
- Your trainer may require a letter of 'medical clearance' from your GP. Please be aware that your GP may charge you for this.

CANCELLATION POLICY

- 48 hours' notice of cancellation is required for all appointments.
- Notice of between 24 and 48 hours will require a 50% payment of the session fee.
- Notice of less than 24 hours will incur full payment of the session fee.

LATENESS POLICY

- If the client is late for a session the session will not be extended and will end at the appointed time.
- If the trainer is late, additional time will be added to the session or to subsequent sessions.

FEE CHARGING POLICY

- Payment for single sessions must be made at the time of booking. Cheques to be made payable to _____
- Block bookings must be paid for in advance, BUT sessions do not have to be booked in advance. However, all sessions must be redeemed within 90 days of purchase.
- All monies paid are non-refundable.

I recognise and understand all the terms and conditions set between my personal trainer and myself and agree to follow all the guidelines set out above.

Client signature:

Print name:

Date:

Trainer signature:

Print name:

Date:

Food Diary

Client name:

	Morning	Lunchtime	Afternoon	Evening
DAY ONE: Date: .... Please give a rough idea of times of day and include all main meals, drinks (including water) and snacks				

Trainer comments:

Physical Activity Readiness Questionnaire (PAR-Q)

If you are between the ages of 15 and 69, the PAR-Q will tell you if you should check with your doctor before you significantly change your physical activity patterns. If you are over 69 years of age and are not used to being very active, check with your doctor. Common sense is your best guide when answering these questions. Please read carefully and answer each one honestly: please tick either YES or NO.

1 Has your doctor ever said you have a heart condition and that you should only do physical activity recommended by a doctor?   Yes ☐ No ☐

2 Do you feel pain in your chest when you do physical activity?   Yes ☐ No ☐

3 In the past month, have you had a chest pain when you were not doing physical activity?   Yes ☐ No ☐

4 Do you lose your balance because of dizziness or do you ever lose consciousness?   Yes ☐ No ☐

5 Do you have a bone or joint problem (for example, back, knee, or hip) that could be made worse by a change in your physical activity?   Yes ☐ No ☐

6 Is your doctor currently prescribing medication for your blood pressure or heart condition?   Yes ☐ No ☐

7 Do you know of **any other reason** why you should not do physical activity?   Yes ☐ No ☐

If yes, please comment:

YES to one or more questions:
You should consult with your doctor to clarify that it is safe for you to become physically active at this current time and in your current state of health.

NO to all questions:
It is reasonably safe for you to participate in physical activity, gradually building up from your current ability level. A fitness appraisal can help determine your ability levels.

Physical Activity Readiness Questionnaire (PAR-Q) *continued*

I have read, understood and accurately completed this questionnaire. I confirm that I am voluntarily engaging in an acceptable level of exercise, and my participation involves a risk of injury.

Signature

Print name

Date

Having answered YES to one of the above, I have sought medical advice and my GP has agreed that I may exercise.

Signature

Date

Note: This physical activity clearance is valid for a maximum of 12 months from the date it is completed and becomes invalid if your condition changes so that you would answer YES to any of the 7 questions.

Short-Term Goals

Name:

Date:

Please list your short-term goals	Goal Date	Date Achieved
1		
2		
3		

What, if any, obstacles do you see yourself encountering?

1

2

3

How will you overcome these obstacles?

1

2

3

Do you have specific concerns regarding the achievability of these goals?

1

2

3

Signature   Date

Long-Term Goals

Name:

Date:

	Please list your long-term goals	Goal Date	Date Achieved
1			
2			
3			

	What, if any, obstacles do you see yourself encountering?
1	
2	
3	

	How will you overcome these obstacles?
1	
2	
3	

	Do you have specific concerns regarding the achievability of these goals?
1	
2	
3	

Signature   Date

INDEX

ACKNOWLEDGEMENTS

My most sincere thanks are due to the following people:

- Clinton McKenzie for starting it all, and for his contribution to this book.
- Danny and Joe Levart, and Sandra Booer, for always being there.
- Dave Cowland for the coaching help.
- Freddie Brown for reviewing the chapter on nutrition and hydration.
- Grant Pritchard for the photos.
- Helena Booer, Etienne Bruce, Joe Levart and Chris McKenzie, for their assistance at the photoshoot.
- John Lissenden, for his editorial help, and for being so open-minded.
- Leigh Bruce and Sol Whyte, for sharing my vision.
- My clients, for the fun and the loyalty.
- My publisher, Charlotte Croft, my editor, Sarah Cole, and my copy-editor, Victoria Chow, for their belief and hard work.
- Ron Tulley for the information on the ABA 'BOX' programme.
- Sally-Ann Cairns for her best-friendship.
- Terry Gillam for being my mentor.
- Tommy Gunn at Gunns MMA Fitness for hosting the photoshoot.